# ENVIRONMENTAL DISASTERS

# EARTH • AT • RISK

# ENVIRONMENTAL DISASTERS

by Rebecca Stefoff

Introduction by
Russell E. Train

Chairman of
the Board of Directors,
World Wildlife Fund and
The Conservation Foundation

CHELSEA HOUSE PUBLISHERS

new york   philadelphia

CHELSEA HOUSE PUBLISHERS

EDITORIAL DIRECTOR: Richard Rennert
EXECUTIVE MANAGING EDITOR: Karyn Gullen Browne
EXECUTIVE EDITOR: Sean Dolan
COPY CHIEF: Robin James
PICTURE EDITOR: Adrian G. Allen
ART DIRECTOR: Robert Mitchell
MANUFACTURING DIRECTOR: Gerald Levine
PRODUCTION COORDINATOR: Marie Claire Cebrián-Ume

EARTH AT RISK
SENIOR EDITOR: Jake Goldberg

Staff for *Environmental Disasters*
EDITORIAL ASSISTANT: Mary B. Sisson
PICTURE RESEARCHER: Villette Harris
SENIOR DESIGNER: Marjorie Zaum
COVER ILLUSTRATOR: Yemi

First Printing

1   3   5   7   9   8   6   4   2

Library of Congress Cataloging-in-Publication Data
Stefoff, Rebecca, 1951–
    Environmental disasters/Rebecca Stefoff; introduction by Russell
E. Train.
        p. cm.—(Earth at risk)
    Includes bibliographical references and index.
    Summary: Discusses causes and ramifications of environmental
disasters using actual disasters as case studies.
    ISBN  0-7910-1584-X
            0-7910-1609-9 (pbk.)
    1. Environmental degradation—Juvenile literature. 2. Natural
disasters—Environmental aspects—Juvenile literature. 3. Natural
disasters—Environmental aspects—Case studies—Juvenile
literature. [1. Natural disasters. 2. Environmental protection.] I.
Title. II. Series.                                              93-8183
GE140.5.S74 1994                                              CIP
363.7—dc20                                                     AC

# C O N T E N T S

# INTRODUCTION

Russell E. Train
Administrator, Environmental Protection Agency, 1973 to
1977; Chairman of the Board of Directors, World Wildlife
Fund and The Conservation Foundation

There is a growing realization that human activities increasingly
are threatening the health of the natural systems that make life possible
on this planet. Humankind has the power to alter nature fundamentally,
perhaps irreversibly.

This stark reality was dramatized in January 1989 when *Time*
magazine named Earth the "Planet of the Year." In the same year, the
Exxon *Valdez* disaster sparked public concern over the effects of human
activity on vulnerable ecosystems when a thick blanket of crude oil
coated the shores and wildlife of Prince William Sound in Alaska. And,
no doubt, the 20th anniversary celebration of Earth Day in April 1990
renewed broad public interest in environmental issues still further. It is
no accident then that many people are calling the years between 1990
and 2000 the "Decade of the Environment."

And this is not merely a case of media hype, for the 1990s will
truly be a time when the people of the planet Earth learn the meaning of
the phrase "everything is connected to everything else" in the natural
and man-made systems that sustain our lives. This will be a period when
more people will understand that burning a tree in Amazonia adversely
affects the global atmosphere just as much as the exhaust from the cars
that fill our streets and expressways.

Central to our understanding of environmental issues is the
need to recognize the complexity of the problems we face and the

relationships between environmental and other needs in our society. Global warming provides an instructive example. Controlling emissions of carbon dioxide, the principal greenhouse gas, will involve efforts to reduce the use of fossil fuels to generate electricity. Such a reduction will include energy conservation and the promotion of alternative energy sources, such as nuclear and solar power.

The automobile contributes significantly to the problem. We have the choice of switching to more energy-efficient autos and, in the longer run, of choosing alternative automotive power systems and relying more on mass transit. This will require different patterns of land use and development, patterns that are less transportation and energy intensive.

In agriculture, rice paddies and cattle are major sources of greenhouse gases. Recent experiments suggest that universally used nitrogen fertilizers may inhibit the ability of natural soil organisms to take up methane, thus contributing tremendously to the atmospheric loading of that gas—one of the major culprits in the global warming scenario.

As one explores the various parameters of today's pressing environmental challenges, it is possible to identify some areas where we have made some progress. We have taken important steps to control gross pollution over the past two decades. What I find particularly encouraging is the growing environmental consciousness and activism by today's youth. In many communities across the country, young people are working together to take their environmental awareness out of the classroom and apply it to everyday problems. Successful recycling and tree-planting projects have been launched as a result of these budding environmentalists who have committed themselves to a cleaner environment. Citizen action, activated by youthful enthusiasm, was largely responsible for the fast-food industry's switch from rainforest to domestic beef, for pledges from important companies in the tuna industry to use fishing techniques that would not harm dolphins, and for the recent announcement by the McDonald's Corporation to phase out polystyrene "clam shell" hamburger containers.

Despite these successes, much remains to be done if we are to make ours a truly healthy environment. Even a short list of persistent issues includes problems such as acid rain, ground-level ozone and smog, and airborne toxins; groundwater protection and nonpoint sources of pollution, such as runoff from farms and city streets; wetlands protection; hazardous waste dumps; and solid waste disposal, waste minimization, and recycling.

Similarly, there is an unfinished agenda in the natural resources area: effective implementation of newly adopted management plans for national forests; strengthening the wildlife refuge system; national park management, including addressing the growing pressure of development on lands surrounding the parks; implementation of the Endangered Species Act; wildlife trade problems, such as that involving elephant ivory; and ensuring adequate sustained funding for these efforts at all levels of government. All of these issues are before us today; most will continue in one form or another through the year 2000.

Each of these challenges to environmental quality and our health requires a response that recognizes the complex nature of the problem. Narrowly conceived solutions will not achieve lasting results. Often it seems that when we grab hold of one part of the environmental balloon, an unsightly and threatening bulge appears somewhere else.

The higher environmental issues arise on the national agenda, the more important it is that we are armed with the best possible knowledge of the economic costs of undertaking particular environmental programs and the costs associated with not undertaking them. Our society is not blessed with unlimited resources, and tough choices are going to have to be made. These should be informed choices.

All too often, environmental objectives are seen as at cross-purposes with other considerations vital to our society. Thus, environmental protection is often viewed as being in conflict with economic growth, with energy needs, with agricultural productions, and so on. The time has come when environmental considerations must be fully integrated into every nation's priorities.

One area that merits full legislative attention is energy efficiency. The United States is one of the least energy efficient of all the industrialized nations. Japan, for example, uses far less energy per unit of gross national product than the United States does. Of course, a country as large as the United States requires large amounts of energy for transportation. However, there is still a substantial amount of excess energy used, and this excess constitutes waste. More fuel-efficient autos and home heating systems would save millions of barrels of oil, or their equivalent, each year. And air pollutants, including greenhouse gases, could be significantly reduced by increased efficiency in industry.

I suspect that the environmental problem that comes closest to home for most of us is the problem of what to do with trash. All over the world, communities are wrestling with the problem of waste disposal. Landfill sites are rapidly filling to capacity. No one wants a trash and garbage dump near home. As William Ruckelshaus, former EPA administrator and now in the waste management business, puts it, "Everyone wants you to pick up the garbage and no one wants you to put it down!"

At the present time, solid waste programs emphasize the regulation of disposal, setting standards for landfills, and so forth. In the decade ahead, we must shift our emphasis from regulating waste disposal to an overall reduction in its volume. We must look at the entire waste stream, including product design and packaging. We must avoid creating waste in the first place. To the greatest extent possible, we should then recycle any waste that is produced. I believe that, while most of us enjoy our comfortable way of life and have no desire to change things, we also know in our hearts that our "disposable society" has allowed us to become pretty soft.

Land use is another domestic issue that might well attract legislative attention by the year 2000. All across the United States, communities are grappling with the problem of growth. All too often, growth imposes high costs on the environment—the pollution of aquifers; the destruction of wetlands; the crowding of shorelines; the loss of wildlife habitat; and the loss of those special places, such as a historic structure or area, that give a community a sense of identity. It is worth noting that growth is not only the product of economic development but of population movement. By the year 2010, for example, experts predict that 75% of all Americans will live within 50 miles of a coast.

It is important to keep in mind that we are all made vulnerable by environmental problems that cross international borders. Of course, the most critical global conservation problems are the destruction of tropical forests and the consequent loss of their biological capital. Some scientists have calculated extinction rates as high as 11 species per hour. All agree that the loss of species has never been greater than at the present time; not even the disappearance of the dinosaurs can compare to today's rate of extinction.

In addition to species extinctions, the loss of tropical forests may represent as much as 20% of the total carbon dioxide loadings to the atmosphere. Clearly, any international approach to the problem of global warming must include major efforts to stop the destruction of forests and to manage those that remain on a renewable basis. Debt for nature swaps, which the World Wildlife Fund has pioneered in Costa Rica, Ecuador, Madagascar, and the Philippines, provide a useful mechanism for promoting such conservation objectives.

Global environmental issues inevitably will become the principal focus in international relations. But the single overriding issue facing the world community today is how to achieve a sustainable balance between growing human populations and the earth's natural systems. If you travel as frequently as I do in the developing countries of Latin America, Africa, and Asia, it is hard to escape the reality that expanding human populations are seriously weakening the earth's resource base. Rampant deforestation, eroding soils, spreading deserts, loss of biological diversity, the destruction of fisheries, and polluted and degraded urban environments threaten to spread environmental impoverishment, particularly in the tropics, where human population growth is greatest.

It is important to recognize that environmental degradation and human poverty are closely linked. Impoverished people desperate for land on which to grow crops or graze cattle are destroying forests and overgrazing even more marginal land. These people become trapped in a vicious downward spiral. They have little choice but to continue to overexploit the weakened resources available to them. Continued abuse of these lands only diminishes their productivity. Throughout the developing world, alarming amounts of land rendered useless by over-grazing and poor agricultural practices have become virtual wastelands, yet human numbers continue to multiply in these areas.

From Bangladesh to Haiti, we are confronted with an increasing number of ecological basket cases. In the Philippines, a traditional focus of U.S. interest, environmental devastation is widespread as deforestation, soil erosion, and the destruction of coral reefs and fisheries combine with the highest population growth rate in Southeast Asia.

Controlling human population growth is the key factor in the environmental equation. World population is expected to at least double to about 11 billion before leveling off. Most of this growth will occur in the poorest nations of the developing world. I would hope that the United States will once again become a strong advocate of international efforts to promote family planning. Bringing human populations into a sustainable balance with their natural resource base must be a vital objective of U.S. foreign policy.

Foreign economic assistance, the program of the Agency for International Development (AID), can become a potentially powerful tool for arresting environmental deterioration in developing countries. People who profess to care about global environmental problems— the loss of biological diversity, the destruction of tropical forests, the greenhouse effect, the impoverishment of the marine environment, and so on—should be strong supporters of foreign aid planning and the principles of sustainable development urged by the World Commission on Environment and Development, the "Brundtland Commission."

If sustainability is to be the underlying element of overseas assistance programs, so too must it be a guiding principle in people's practices at home. Too often we think of sustainable development only in terms of the resources of other countries. We have much that we can and should be doing to promote long-term sustainability in our own resource management. The conflict over our own rainforests, the old growth forests of the Pacific Northwest, illustrates this point.

The decade ahead will be a time of great activity on the environmental front, both globally and domestically. I sincerely believe we will be tested as we have been only in times of war and during the Great Depression. We must set goals for the year 2000 that will challenge both the American people and the world community.

Despite the complexities ahead, I remain an optimist. I am confident that if we collectively commit ourselves to a clean, healthy environment we can surpass the achievements of the 1980s and meet the serious challenges that face us in the coming decades. I hope that today's students will recognize their significant role in and responsibility for bringing about change and will rise to the occasion to improve the quality of our global environment.

*Volcanic eruptions are dramatic natural disasters that human beings can do little to prevent, but the burning of forests and the polluting of the air by human activity can be just as devastating.*

chapter 1

# WHAT IS AN ENVIRONMENTAL DISASTER?

On May 6, 1987, one of the worst forest fires in history started when a young man spilled some gasoline in northeastern China. Eighteen-year-old Wang Yufeng had been hired as a temporary worker in the Chinese government's forest service. He lived in Hebei province, east of Beijing, the capital of China, but he had been visiting a cousin who lived in the town of Xilinji in the northeastern province of Heilongjiang. Wang had no money to buy a train ticket for his return to Hebei, so his cousin's wife arranged for him to work in the forest service for a few weeks. There is nothing extraordinary about a teenager getting a temporary job to earn a little money, but in Wang's case the consequences were to be enormous.

On May 6 Wang was assigned to work as a brush cutter. His job was to go over ground that had been logged, cutting down weeds and bushes so that the other five members of his work team could plant new trees. He was given a gaso-line-powered cutter that consisted of a framework of metal tubes with a spinning blade at one end; he operated it by bracing the frame against his body and swinging the blade from side to side. The cutter's engine, like that of a lawn mower or outboard motor, started when the operator pulled a cord. The gas tank was full, but Wang was given a spare can of gas so that he could work all day without returning to the forest service headquarters.

Rules governed the use of the cutters and other forestry tools. These tools were supposed to be operated only by trained workers, and their gas tanks were supposed to be filled only over concrete slabs or on roads or highways that had been cleared of vegetation. Perhaps Wang ignored the rules, or perhaps he never learned them; it is not known whether he received any training at all. But when he refilled the empty gas tank from his spare fuel can, he did so in a dry, brushy field, and he spilled gasoline on the outside of the tank, the frame of the cutter, and the ground. The first pull of the starting cord lit a spark that ignited the gasoline not only inside the engine but on the frame.

Suddenly the cutter was engulfed in flames. The panicky Wang dropped the cutter to the ground. Immediately the fire spread to the gasoline he had spilled, and then to nearby tufts of dry, brittle grass and brush. Crackling across this tinder, the flames quickly reached the nearby forest of birch, larch, and aspen trees, which began blazing. The Great Black Dragon Fire had begun.

Within a few days this fire would consume more than 3 million acres of trees—between one-sixth and one-fifth of China's total remaining forest cover. It would kill 220 people, injure 250 more, and destroy whole communities, including Xilinji, the town where Wang Yufeng had been staying. Firefighters and army units would battle heroically to control the fire and keep it from devouring all of North China's trees. Meanwhile,

*A street in Messina, Italy, after an earthquake in 1908.*

the heat, dust storms, and plumes of black smoke created by the fire plagued Beijing and were felt as far away as Korea and Alaska.

The Black Dragon River is the traditional Chinese name for the Amur River. It runs along the border between Siberia, in eastern Russia, and the northeastern corner of China, the region once known as Manchuria. A huge conifer forest—the largest nontropical forest in the world—stretches along both sides of the Amur and covers much of southeastern Siberia, Heilongjiang province in China, and North Korea. Forest fires are not uncommon in the area, especially in Siberia, where little attempt is made to control fires that occur naturally as the result of lightning strikes. China, which is rapidly using up its timber resources, has embarked on many programs to protect or replant its dwindling forests. These programs have not been very successful, but they do show that forest conservation is an official priority in China.

At the time of the Great Black Dragon Fire in Heilongjiang, several even larger fires were raging in the Siberian part of the forest, north of the Amur. No effort was made by the Russian authorities to curb them. Satellite photos suggest that the Siberian fires destroyed between 9 million and 15 million acres of trees. The total loss of woodland on both sides of the river may have been 18 million acres, or more than 28,000 square miles. In other words, an area half the size of New England, or nearly as large as Scotland, was reduced to charred stumps.

Wang Yufeng, the hapless forester who started the Heilongjiang fire, received a sentence of six and a half years in prison for negligence. The Chinese government, with aid and advice from Canada and other nations, began making plans to reseed the devastated areas. But the long-term consequences of the fire remain unknown.

Some experts fear that the forest will not be able to renew itself, particularly if there is another large fire. Part of the problem lies in reduced rainfall. A burned-over forest's power to generate and trap moisture is decreased, and therefore less rain tends to fall on forest areas that have been burned. In turn, decreased rainfall impairs the forest's ability to regenerate itself, and a vicious cycle of erosion and drying out may begin. One result of the fire may to be accelerate the desertification that has been going on in northwestern China for a long time. If so, desertlike conditions will spread eastward, and the mountains and valleys of Heilongjiang, once covered with trees, will gradually become barren. In addition, it is impossible to calculate the effects that the Great Black Dragon Fire may have had upon global weather patterns. The addition of millions of tons of ash to the world's atmosphere could have altered patterns of wind, temperature, and rainfall halfway around the world from the Amur River.

## NATURAL AND ENVIRONMENTAL DISASTERS

Together the fires of Heilongjiang and Siberia made up the largest forest fire on record. Yet should the fires be considered "environmental disasters"? Or were they natural cataclysms of the sort that are sometimes called "acts of God"? The Siberian portion of the fire was far larger than the Chinese portion—the Siberian fire, in effect, was more disastrous than the Chinese fire. But an important difference between the two fires lies in the concepts of cause and preventability.

No one knows for sure what caused the Siberian fires; most likely they were started by lightning. But the Chinese fire had a human origin. It is the fact of human responsibility that makes the Great Black Dragon Fire an environmental disaster.

*This mile-wide crater in Arizona was formed when a meteorite 600 feet in diameter struck the earth. Such asteroid strikes were more common in the early history of the earth and may have altered the planet's climate.*

Danger and destruction are part of the natural order of the world. But damage that is caused by human activity—damage to the environment that *could* have been prevented—is not part of nature's cycle of destruction and renewal. Such damage causes stresses on the earth from which it may not be able to recover, stresses that may have unpredictable results.

Forest fires occur all the time without human cause. Some forestry experts believe that it is better to let such fires burn than to try to put them out, because forest ecosystems have evolved over millions of years to survive and even to benefit from natural fires. Forest fires caused by humans, however, must be considered disasters. They are unnecessary and preventable, and they may push a forest ecosystem past the point of recovery. But at least they are no different in kind from fires that are caused naturally by lightning or by red-hot volcanic lava. Other kinds of environmental disasters have no counterparts in nature. Oil spills, nuclear reactor leaks, and explosions of poisonous chemicals are caused by people, not by natural processes or phenomena. These stresses are environmentally disastrous, both for the natural world and for its human inhabitants.

A natural disaster may have a catastrophic effect on human life and property, but it is usually thought of as being beyond the scope of human beings to prevent or control. Such events as tidal waves, earthquakes, volcanic eruptions, naturally ignited fires, hurricanes, tornadoes, floods, and landslides fall into this category. All of these are caused by natural processes. People may try to predict them, as when meteorologists track hurricanes and issue storm warnings. People may also try to limit the effects of such disasters, by building dams and dikes to hold back floodwater, by organizing firefighting teams, and by reinforcing skyscrapers to withstand earthquakes. But for the most part natural disasters themselves are beyond human control.

An environmental disaster, on the other hand, refers to massive or serious damage to the environment that was caused, or at least made worse, by human activity. An environmental disaster is a destructive event that could have been prevented by greater knowledge, more thoughtful individual actions, or better laws and regulations. It is tempting to blame environmental disasters on large, impersonal organizations such as governments, oil companies, and chemical manufacturers. The case of Wang Yufeng shows, however, that ordinary citizens, far away from corporate boardrooms and government offices, can also cause environmental disasters—and that all individuals share responsibility for preventing them.

## SUDDEN DEATH AND SLOW FUSES

The term *environmental disaster* embraces a wide variety of events. Some of them are specific incidents that occur at a single point in time, such as the oil spill from the Exxon tanker *Valdez*, which struck a reef off Alaska on March 24, 1989, or the explosion of the Soviet nuclear reactor at Chernobyl on April 26, 1986. Other environmental disasters are less specific. They are the result of dozens or even thousands of occurrences whose effects build up over time. One such slow-building disaster was caused by the storing of toxic chemical wastes in Love Canal, New York, where residents suffered from increased rates of birth defects caused by 40 years' worth of poisons seeping into their soil and water. Delayed or slow disasters like Love Canal are like

*This elderly Indian woman is one of many demonstrators protesting the inadequate compensation given to victims of methyl isocyanate gas released from a Union Carbide chemical plant in Bhopal, India, in 1984.*

time bombs whose fuses have been set: the explosion may not come right away, but it *will* come.

Some environmental disasters are immediately visible, as when clouds of poisonous gas hover over a city after an explosion in a chemical plant. The effects of other disasters are delayed, or perhaps spread over long periods. For example, smog killed 4,000 people in London in a four-day period in 1952; another 700 Londoners perished from smog poisoning during five days in 1962. The "killer smog," as it was called, was caused by a variety of factors, including weather, automobile exhausts, and factory emissions, that built up over time. It was a cumulative disaster, not a single event, although the deaths occurred within a short period.

Many environmental disasters create both sudden-death *and* slow-fuse risks. An oil spill, for example, may kill birds, fish, and sea mammals within hours or days, but it may also have a long-term effect on the ecological health of a large undersea area. Oil settling to the bottom of the sea may prevent plant growth, which in turn may cause fish populations to decline over a period of years. Similarly, an accident at a nuclear reactor may cause immediate deaths or injuries, but its long-term effects may be even more serious: increased rates of cancer and other diseases among people who live in the region, contamination of crops by radioactive debris scattered over a wide area, or leakage of radioactive fluids into underground water sources.

All environmental disasters, however, have one thing in common: they hurt the environment. They may hurt or kill many people, but their baneful effects are not limited to human suffering. A train wreck that kills 400 passengers is a disaster, but a train wreck that spills acid into a river system is an environmental disaster. Environmental disasters may be large or small. The small ones, though, add up. Emptying a can of kerosene into a storm drain may seem insignificant compared with the spectacular ravages of the *Valdez* oil spill, but enough cans down enough storm drains can do as much damage as any badly steered supertanker.

Some environmental disasters are so big and so gradual that they are difficult to comprehend. Global warming, overpopulation, air and water pollution, the onrushing extinction of thousands of species of plants and animals, the destruction of the tropical rainforests, and the desertification of fertile land are all serious problems that could threaten humankind's continued existence, yet these disasters are difficult to keep in mind on a day-to-day basis. In their 1989 book *New World, New Mind*, neurobiologist Robert Ornstein and population scientist Paul Ehrlich suggest that human perceptions and reflexes are brilliantly adapted to recognize and react to sudden, immediate changes in the environment but not so well suited to perceiving and acting on very small, slow changes. A person who smells smoke or sees flames, for example, will probably leave the room and call for help. But that same person may not notice that each summer seems a tiny bit hotter and drier than the one before—and if he does notice it, he may not feel impelled to take action.

*A 19th-century artist's fanciful vision of the earth being torn apart by a collision with a comet.*

*Tugboats pull the damaged Exxon* Valdez *through Prince William Sound in Alaska two weeks after the supertanker struck a reef and released its cargo of oil into the Sound.*

Most of us find it easier to focus on specific incidents than on general conditions. The topic of nuclear safety may seem boringly vague, but the Chernobyl reactor explosion has the power to grab our emotions and make us think. Industrial accidents sound technical and dull, but the tragedy at Bhopal reminds us of what is at stake in the chemical industry. This is why we study environmental disasters. These events are not just horror stories from the past. They are also tools for evaluating our present environmental policies—and perhaps guides to preventing further, even greater disasters in the years to come.

Workers sample the contents of 55-gallon drums of toxic substances as part of efforts to clean up this hazardous waste site in Hamilton, Ohio. At the time the picture was taken, the site still held 10,000 such drums.

## B A D   C H E M I S T R Y

Bhopal is a city of 800,000 people in central India. Quite a few of its Hindu and Muslim inhabitants work in the many large industrial factories that have been built in the city. The factories bring jobs and income to the region, but the people of Bhopal have paid a high price for those jobs. In 1984, Bhopal became the site of history's worst industrial accident.

Union Carbide, one of many American companies that manufacture chemicals in India, had built a plant in Bhopal to make pesticides. Early in the morning of December 3, 1984, a valve broke on a storage tank at that plant. Thirty tons of a highly poisonous chemical called methyl isocyanate (MIC) leaked from the tank and billowed out over the city in an acrid, low-lying cloud. Night workers at the plant noticed the leak when their eyes began watering, but they could do nothing to control it; most of them fled in terror. The cloud spread and moved across the city.

Soon people in the crowded slums and wealthy suburbs of Bhopal woke sneezing, coughing, and vomiting. Before long every road out of the city was clogged with people fleeing by car, bus, ox cart, and on foot. Their desperate exodus was the largest unplanned evacuation on record. Some of those who could not outrun the creeping MIC cloud choked to death on their vomit; others went blind or suffered permanent damage to their hearts, lungs, or nervous or digestive systems. More than 2,500 people died that morning, and 17,000 more were permanently injured, many of them blinded. Altogether 200,000 people or more were exposed to the MIC, and even those who appeared to suffer no ill effects at the time may be at risk for long-term complications such as cancer.

The Bhopal disaster caused a storm of protest and outrage around the world. Arguments over the exact cause of the leak—and over who is ultimately responsible—continued into the 1990s. Investigators agree, however, that poor design and inadequate maintenance made the plant unsafe, "an accident waiting to happen," as reporters called it. Furthermore, the plant lacked basic safety devices that could have contained the leak and saved lives.

Today about 80,000 chemicals are used in various industrial and manufacturing processes. Some 37,000 of these chemicals are pesticides—that is, chemicals used to kill or control pests, such as insects and rodents. Contrary to popular belief, very few of these 80,000 chemicals have been fully tested to

*The spraying of pesticides poisons soils and sources of fresh water, but it is a slow process and people have difficulty seeing it as a dramatic environmental disaster comparable to an oil spill or a nuclear reactor failure.*

determine their effect on human or environmental health. In many cases the chemicals are known to be deadly but are used anyway because they are useful in the production of everything from paper and plastic to fertilizer and furniture.

Modern industrial civilization produces and consumes enormous amounts of these chemicals. The United States alone has about 12,000 chemical manufacturing plants and 400,000 chemical storage facilities, each of which is potentially a disaster site; in addition, millions of businesses such as dry cleaners, paper mills, auto body shops, and photo labs use chemicals, many of them hazardous to human health.

Pesticides have been linked to cancer and birth defects. Dioxin, the most toxic chemical known, causes cancer, birth defects, and skin disease; lead and other metals cause nervous system damage, liver and kidney damage, and learning disabilities; benzene, used in the manufacture of medicines and detergents, is linked to leukemia; and chlorinated solvents, used to remove grease in many industrial processes and also found in household products such as furniture strippers, cause lung, liver, kidney, and heart damage, and may cause birth defects. Polychlorinated biphenyls (PCBs) occur in electronic components, fluorescent lights, and hydraulic fluids. They can contaminate soil and accumulate in living tissue. Their health effects are not known for certain but they have been linked to damage of the skin, stomach, and intestines. PCBs may also cause cancer: Japanese people who ate fish that had accidentally been contaminated with PCBs developed higher-than-normal rates of stomach and liver cancer. Tragically, much of what we know about the toxic effects of chemicals has been learned from accidents like this one and the one at Bhopal.

There have been other serious chemical accidents before and after Bhopal. In 1976, an explosion at a chemical plant in Seveso, Italy, released dioxin into the air and caused 700 people to be evacuated from their homes. Less than a year after the Bhopal disaster, another Union Carbide plant—this one in Institute, West Virginia—had a chemical leak. One hundred and thirty-five people were injured.

Switzerland is often thought of as a pristine, healthy country, but it is just as subject to chemical hazards as the rest of the world. In November 1986, disaster struck when a warehouse in Basel, Switzerland, caught on fire. The fire released 30 tons of pesticides into the Rhine River. Flowing through the heart of in-dustrialized Europe, the Rhine had become severely polluted in earlier decades. The International Commission for the Protection of the Rhine was formed to clean up the river and protect it from further damage. The commission had made much progress; the Rhine was recovering. But the accident in Basel undid the com-mission's good work, creating a huge slick of poison that floated downstream on the surface of the water. A 120-mile stretch of the Rhine was ravaged—all plant and animal life, including micro-scopic creatures, was exterminated. Half a million fish and 150,000 eels perished, and commercial fishers were forced out of business. The river remained biologically dead for several years, and drinking water in Germany and the Netherlands was contaminated with the pesticides.

Polychlorinated biphenyls, or PCBs, are highly poison-ous chemicals commonly used as insulation in electri-cal devices, but their use is being phased out because of their toxicity.

In the wake of the Bhopal disaster, Americans grew concerned about the potential for chemical accidents in their own country. The Environmental Protection Agency (EPA) commissioned a study by independent consultants, who found that 6,928 accidents with toxic chemicals had occurred in the United States from 1980 through the middle of 1985. These mishaps had killed 138 people, injured 4,717, and caused the evacuation of a total of 200,000 people.

Three-quarters of these accidents took place at manufacturing plants or storage facilities; the rest occurred while chemicals were being shipped, usually by truck or train. Some accidents were caused by mechanical failures, such as leaking tanks, broken valves and gauges, and overdue repairs. Others were caused by human error. They covered a wide geographic range and a broad spectrum of chemical hazards. For example, a pesticide leak injured 3 people in New Jersey; a chlorine cloud escaped from a chemical plant and descended upon a high school football game in Niagara Falls, New York, killing 1 person and injuring 76; nitric acid exploded in Mississippi, killing 3 and injuring 61; ammonia from industrial cooling systems killed 4 people in San Antonio, Texas, and injured another 270 in businesses nationwide; and a solvent leak in New York City caused 40 injuries.

Recognizing that the tragedy at Bhopal had been worsened by the plant's location in the center of a densely populated area, the Congressional Research Service examined the siting of America's chemical plants. Investigators found that more than 6,300 chemical plants and related facilities were located in the country's 25 largest urban areas, home to 75% of all Americans. Northern New Jersey—the center of the East Coast megalopolis that stretches from Boston to Washington, D.C.—had 800 plants. A chemical accident in the empty wilderness would be a disaster, but at least it would probably claim few lives. The concentration of U.S. plants in population centers, however, suggests that a major chemical accident would very likely cause a high number of casualties.

Summing up the risk to Americans, a chemical engineer and hazardous chemicals specialist named Roger Batstone told the *New York Times* in 1985, "This country has been very lucky it has not had a major chemical accident killing a lot of people. Those who try to minimize the hazards are totally wrong. And if there aren't many changes in the next couple of years, there probably will be a major accident here."

There *have* been some changes. Stimulated partly by the sobering events at Bhopal and partly by the growing recognition that Americans, too, were at risk, Congress addressed the issue of chemical safety and revised a 1980 law called the Comprehensive Environmental Response, Compensation, and Liability Act (called CERCLA or Superfund). The act was designed to create a federal framework for solving toxic chemical problems. Although Superfund is often thought of as a plan for identifying and cleaning up hazardous waste sites such as leaking landfills, it also laid out guidelines for the cleanup of toxic spills and the handling of chemical accidents. In 1986, when Superfund was amended, Congress also passed the Emergency Planning and Community Right-to-Know Act, usually called simply Right-to-Know. Some environmental activists think that Right-to-Know is one of the public's most powerful weapons in the battle to prevent further chemical disasters.

The Right-to-Know Act was designed to protect the public from unpleasant surprises. Before the act was passed, chemical

*In Afton, North Carolina, police confront demonstrators angry over the dumping of toxic PCB compounds into local landfills.*

manufacturers and other businesses were not required to tell the public what chemicals they used, or how these chemicals were handled. The act requires businesses that use toxic chemicals to notify their communities about the chemicals used and the amounts of these substances that are discharged into the environment during routine operations or in accidents. The idea behind the law is that people have the right to know what sorts of hazardous materials are being transported, handled, or stored in their communities. Lawmakers felt that if the chemical industry was forced to go public with information about spills, emissions, and accidents, chemical companies would voluntarily tighten up their safety procedures. If they did not do so, community groups would know what they were doing and could take action against them.

To some extent the Right-to-Know Act has had the desired effect. Companies both large and small have cleaned up their acts after their dismal environmental records were made public. One example is the giant chemical manufacturing company Monsanto. In compliance with the Right-to-Know Act, the company monitored its accident and emission records at 35 U.S. plants in 1987. Company officials were dismayed to learn that Monsanto had released 374 million tons of toxic chemicals into the air, water, and ground during one year. In 1988 the chairman of the company pledged to reduce air emissions by 90% by 1993.

Perhaps the most important feature of the Right-to-Know Act is that it requires chemical industry officials to form committees with federal, state, and local authorities and community groups. These committees are responsible for developing emergency plans that spell out how to deal with chemical accidents. The plans are supposed to identify every site that uses any of 402 toxic chemicals cited by the EPA, and they must include details of emergency response procedures, including evacuation routes, appropriate medical treatments, and the role of police and fire units.

The emergency planning aspect of the Right-to-Know Act has not been uniformly enforced. Many communities do not yet have emergency response committees; some companies have not released the necessary information. But at least the act gives community groups and activist organizations a tool for prying information out of reluctant companies. It has given new strength

In the hallway ceiling of this Harlem, New York, elementary school, inspectors have exposed the poisonous asbestos insulation that led to the school's closing.

*Workers in protective clothing test the contents of waste drums at an abandoned paint factory in Phoenixville, Pennsylvania.*

to grass-roots groups fighting to clean up their communities and keep them safe. A number of other countries either have enacted similar laws or are planning to introduce them in the future.

In 1985 Lee Thomas, an EPA administrator, observed that several factors could help reduce the risk of another Bhopal. These include the willingness of companies to inform the public about the toxic substances they use; a well-developed emergency response plan in every community; more and better safety training in the chemical industry, including programs that use computerized simulations of disasters, similar to the flight simulators used to train pilots; and an emphasis on safety as a top industrial priority, even if it makes plant operations more expensive. Even if all of these conditions are met, however, the potential for disaster will exist as long as toxic chemicals are made and used. News broadcasts and newspapers will continue to include items like this announcement, which appeared in the December 28, 1992, issue of *USA Today:*

> CHEMICAL SPILL: About 400 Titusville, Fla., residents re-turned home—29 hours after being evacuated Saturday because a leak of phosphorous trichloride at a nearby Pharmco Laboratories facility mixed with rain to form a dangerous gas cloud over the area.

*A young man sits dejectedly outside a section of the Niagara Falls, New York, community of Love Canal, which is fenced off because of toxic chemical leakage from an old landfill.*

chapter    3

TOXIC    TIME    BOMBS

Chemical accidents are not the only type of environmental disasters caused by toxic substances. Another type of disaster is more common and perhaps more deadly. Hundreds of thousands of people—as well as the rest of the biosphere— have been slowly poisoned over long periods of time by chemicals that have leaked or been dumped into the land, sea, and air. These slow-leak accidents do not happen in a single, dramatic moment like industrial leaks and spills, but their long-term effects may be far worse, simply because of their great numbers. In the United States and around the world, millions of toxic time bombs are quietly ticking away. No one knows how many of them will explode, or when.

The cats of Minamata alerted the world to the dangers of slow, long-term chemical poisoning in the 1950s. Minamata is a city on the southeast coast of Japan. Traditionally its economy was based on fishing. During the 1940s and 1950s, some industries, including chemical companies, were established there. But something strange began happening in the 1950s. The city's cats—who fed on booty from the fishing boats and fish markets— began to sicken and die. Their deaths were not easy: the cats were wracked by bone-twisting convulsions and spasms. Many of them drowned themselves in the sea.

Then people started getting sick and dying. Investigators found that both the cats and people were suffering from mercury poisoning. Mercury is a liquid metal that has a number of industrial uses. It can be absorbed through the skin and in some forms is highly toxic. Mercury poisoning can be acute or sudden if a significant dose is swallowed at one time; or it can be chronic if exposure occurs in relatively small doses over a long period of time. The symptoms of mercury poisoning include damage to the mouth, gums, intestinal tract, kidneys, and nervous system; anemia; and paralysis. Severe cases can be fatal.

The feline and human inhabitants of Minamata had one thing in common: they both ate a lot of fish caught in local waters. Without knowing it, they had been steadily consuming lethal doses of mercury. For some time a local chemical company had been dumping its waste—including a compound that contained mercury—right into the bay. In all 700 people were killed. Another 9,000 were crippled. The local fishing industry was destroyed; no one wanted fish from Minamata. Thirty years later, as a 1987 article in the *Washington Post* reported, Minamata had still not recovered from the emotional and economic ravages of what came to be called Minamata disease.

The United States had been planting its own toxic time bombs. The most notorious of these was in the town of Niagara Falls, located in western New York near the Canadian border and the famous waterfall. One neighborhood in Niagara Falls was called Love Canal; it had been built on the site of a canal designed in the 1890s by a man named William T. Love. The canal was never finished, and digging ended in 1920. For the next 30 years, the abandoned ditch was used as a dump. The U.S. Army deposited waste there, and so did the city of Niagara Falls. But the principal dumpers were local chemical companies, particularly Hooker Chemical and the Olin Corporation. Between them they filled the ditch with barrels holding at least 40,000 tons of waste. More than half of this waste was toxic; it included carcinogens, or cancer-causing agents, such as benzene and dioxin.

By the 1950s, the American economy was booming, especially in industrial towns like Niagara Falls. Developers looked for land on which to build homes. They filled Love Canal with earth, covering the rusting metal drums of chemical waste, and built houses and a school on the site. The Love Canal neighborhood was born.

In the 1970s, people who lived in Love Canal began to complain of strange, unpleasant odors in the neighborhood. Some residents found peculiar, foul-smelling sludge seeping through their basement walls. In 1976, researchers found high concentrations of polychlorinated biphenyls (PCBs), extremely toxic chemicals, in Love Canal's storm sewers. The old dump was leaking. Horror stories began to mount: babies were being born with two sets of teeth, or with heart defects, or mentally retarded. The neighborhood's rates of epilepsy, miscarriage, leukemia, cancer, birth defects, and liver and nervous system diseases were far above the national average. In 1978 the New York Department of Health recommended that pregnant women and young children be evacuated from Love Canal. Two years later the federal government declared Love Canal a disaster area and evacuated more than 900 families.

More than a quarter of a billion dollars has been spent cleaning up the mess at Love Canal. The chemical companies were found responsible and ordered to pay for the cleanup, but the government ended up footing a large part of the bill. The school and 300 houses that stood directly above the disposal site were destroyed. Some of the toxic waste was put into secure storage facilities. Some of it was incinerated with high-temperature torches, a process that turns toxic material into less harmful waste that can be put into landfills. In 1988 the federal government and the Centers for Disease Control in Atlanta declared that the cleanup was successful and that people could once again live in the neighborhood, which was renamed Black Creek Village. Although many environmentalists object to resettlement, claiming that toxins remain in Love Canal's soil and water, a few families began moving back into the stricken neighborhood in 1990.

Around the time the cleanup of Love Canal was getting underway, another community was being turned into a ghost town by chemical waste. This time the victim was Times Beach, a small Missouri town. During the 1970s, the town had hired a contractor to spread oil on unpaved roads to keep the dust down. That contractor also worked as a waste hauler for a chemical plant. The same tank truck that hauled chemical sludge was used to carry the oil for the roads, and the residue of the sludge contaminated the oil. For several summers the roads around Times Beach were repeatedly covered with oil that contained lethal dioxin. In 1982, responding to public alarm about the health hazards posed by dioxin, the government declared Times Beach unfit for habitation. Its residents were moved elsewhere and the town was abandoned.

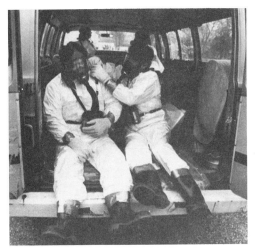

*Two Environmental Protection Agency workers adjust their protective clothing prior to testing for dioxin in the soil of the St. Louis, Missouri, suburb of Times Beach.*

Although Love Canal and Times Beach are similar in some ways, there is one crucial difference. During the 1930s and 1940s, when much of the dumping at Love Canal took place, few people had any idea that chemical waste could be deadly. Scientific studies of the dangers of pesticides and other chemicals were just beginning, and they were not widely accepted by industry, government, or the public. Companies that dumped their waste onto the landscape during those years were careless and irresponsible, but perhaps they did not knowingly and deliberately endanger public health. By the 1970s, however, the dangers of dioxin and other chemicals were well known. The destruction of Times Beach could have been prevented if the chemical company and the contractor had followed ordinarily thoughtful safety procedures.

Times Beach and Love Canal are not alone. Many other communities in the United States have been poisoned by chemical waste. One of them is Jacksonville, Arkansas, a small city 12 miles from the state capital of Little Rock. Some residents call their town Dioxinville. It contains the Vertac chemical plant, which has been closed and locked since 1985. In the years before it shut down, the plant produced tens of thousands of barrels of toxic waste, including a great deal of dioxin, which was casually stored on the plant site. Piles of rusting barrels leaked their contents onto the ground; a 20-foot-tall pile of dioxin-contaminated sludge was nicknamed Vertac Mountain. At the time it was closed, the plant site contained enough toxic waste to cover 20 football fields to a depth of three feet.

Not all the toxins remained in the plant. A significant quantity soaked through the earth into the groundwater. Jacksonville's sewers and city dumps, local creeks, part of a nearby Air Force base, and the plant site itself were contaminated. The Environmental Protection Agency called the Vertac plant "one of the most serious uncontrolled hazardous waste sites in the U.S."

Cancer, birth defects, and sudden infant deaths have occurred at higher than normal rates in Jacksonville. A director of the National Toxics Campaign said of Jacksonville, "This is one of the most serious public health disasters in the United States." Sixty-five residents who claimed personal injury and wrongful death won a settlement from Vertac, but the toxic brew continued to bubble while Vertac, the EPA, and the state and federal governments argued over who should pay to clean up the site and how it should be done. A reporter who visited the town in 1988 was advised by a former resident, "Just don't touch the food, drink the water, or even wash your hands in Jacksonville."

Throughout the world, toxins quietly do their harmful work. In the former Soviet Union and the Soviet-dominated nations of eastern Europe, where rapid industrialization was a high priority after World War II, toxic contamination is widespread and severe. Waste was often heedlessly dropped into rivers or left in unshielded dumps. Whole towns in Poland and Russia are uninhabitable because of chemical poisoning. The eastern part of Germany—formerly the separate state of East Germany—is a toxic mess because the East Germans allowed other countries to dump their toxic wastes there for a fee.

For years England dumped its wastes down old mine shafts, from which toxins found their way into groundwater and the offshore sea. In the United States, petroleum and chemical plants are densely concentrated along an 85-mile stretch of the Mississippi River between Baton Rouge and New Orleans, Louisiana. Industrial boosters call this the Petrochemical Corridor; environmentalists call it Cancer Alley. In Brazil, the corridor between the cities of Rio de Janeiro and São Paulo is the most heavily industrialized part of the country—and the most polluted. Companies there dump their wastes with little regulation. Toxic levels of metals such as cadmium, chromium, and zinc have been found in the offshore waters and in local streams. The rapid growth of the chemical industry in China and India, together with lack of regulation and inadequate antipollution enforcement, has created serious toxic contamination at many sites in those countries.

Nor is toxic contamination limited to countries with chemical industries of their own. In the United States and other industrialized nations, a combination of citizen outrage and stricter disposal laws has closed many dumps and landfills to the producers of toxic waste. But waste must go somewhere, and some cities and corporations have found that it is easier and cheaper to ship it overseas than to dispose of it at home. So they send it to another country, where it may be burned, stored in tanks, or buried in a landfill. The process is called Third World dumping, because many of the host countries are developing nations in the Third World, where knowledge of environmental hazards and the passage of laws to prevent them often lags behind the more developed countries.

Some host countries have accepted the wastes because they are eager to have the disposal fees, but in many cases the host countries do not know exactly what they are getting, or how dangerous it may be. Many nations that were once willing to accept waste are now fighting to resist it. When Nigeria discovered in 1988 that Italy was dumping hazardous materials in a Nigerian port, the angry Nigerians threatened to execute the Italians who were responsible. That same year the Organization of African Unity urged its member nations to ban imports of hazardous wastes from the industrial world, and some African nations have responded with stricter import regulations. In 1989, in an effort to curb dangerous or illegal international shipments of hazardous substances, the United Nations Environment Program adopted a treaty calling for tighter regulations on such shipments. The World Bank also declared that it would not provide loans for aid projects that might result in the international shipment of hazardous waste.

Akin to the problem of Third World dumping is the widespread practice by American and other companies of making and selling products in other countries that are banned in the United States. For example, in many parts of the world DDT is still used to kill insects. Although it is highly toxic and has been banned in the United States since the early 1970s, U.S. and

*At Times Beach, Missouri, trucks loaded with dioxin-contaminated debris await a judge's order to remove the material to a landfill for burial.*

European companies continue to manufacture it and sell it abroad. Not only do such practices contribute to chemical pollution in other countries, but many foods grown in those countries are sold in the United States. Studies have shown that imported fruits and other agricultural products are often contaminated with pesticides.

### REGULATING TOXIC WASTE

It is impossible to say how many toxic waste sites there are in the United States alone. Estimates vary, but in 1987 the General Accounting Office of Congress declared that there were 425,000 hazardous waste sites in the country. In 1988 the EPA issued a summary: at least 29,000 highly toxic waste sites;

180,000 ponds, pits, or lagoons containing toxic chemicals; 16,500 municipal or private landfills; and thousands of injection wells in which wastes have been stored underground. The Congressional Research Service of the Library of Congress has estimated a total of 300,000 hazardous waste dumps across the country. Some of the worst sites belong to the federal government. There are also 5 million or so underground gasoline and oil storage tanks, many of which are cracked and leaking.

As part of a wave of environmental legislation in the 1970s and 1980s, the U.S. Congress passed several laws designed to clean up the worst of these sites and prevent new ones from being created. The Federal Insecticide, Fungicide, and Rodenticide Act (FIFRA), passed in 1972, regulates the manufacture, sale, and use of the pesticides that are used—primarily by the agriculture industry—to kill insects, fungi, and rodents. FIFRA requires the EPA to test all known pesticides for health effects, but as of the early 1990s fewer than half the compounds in use had been tested.

The Safe Drinking Water Act (SDWA) regulates contaminants in water sources. Passed in 1974 and updated in 1986, it sets limits called maximum contaminant levels (MCLs) on the amount of harmful substances that can be present in public drinking water. It also includes some provisions to protect groundwater sources from future contamination by waste  disposal, but this preventive aspect of the law has not been fully enacted.

Congress passed two important waste regulation laws in 1976. The Resource Conservation and Recovery Act (RCRA), designed to keep new Love Canals from coming into being, is the primary law that governs the handling of hazardous waste. It requires any business that produces, transports, or stores hazardous waste to obtain a permit from the EPA and to follow safety procedures set by the EPA. Regulation under RCRA has certainly improved the toxic waste situation in the United States, but environmentalists point to several problems with the act. For one thing, RCRA could be used to force industry to reduce the amount of hazardous waste it produces, but instead the EPA's emphasis has been on treating the waste once it has been made. For another, not all scientists agree that the safety standards set by the EPA are sufficiently rigorous. Finally, violations of RCRA regulations abound. The EPA estimates that only 44% to 57% of all hazardous waste facilities follow the regulations; in one study, the General Accounting Office of Congress learned that EPA inspectors assigned to uncover RCRA violations missed a significant number of these violations.

The Toxic Substances Control Act (TSCA) also dates from 1976. It requires chemical manufacturers to give the EPA information about new chemicals they plan to produce. TSCA gives the EPA the power to limit or ban the use of any substance that "presents or will present an unreasonable risk of injury to health or the environment." TSCA has produced a mass of complicated laboratory studies and piles of paperwork, but many observers feel that its potential for keeping toxins out of the waste stream has barely been tapped.

In 1980, the year Love Canal was declared a federal disaster area, Congress passed the Comprehensive Environmental Response, Compensation, and Liability Act (CERCLA). This law is generally called Superfund because it set aside a fund of $1.6 billion for cleaning up toxic waste sites. Superfund directed the EPA to draw up a list of the nation's hazardous waste sites. By

1990 the EPA had identified more than 26,000 such sites; 1,224 of these were considered severely contaminated.

Superfund has been plagued with scandals, mismanagement of funds, and poor decision making. Critics claim that the EPA has acted slowly and ineffectively: in the act's first five years, only six cleanups were completed, and one of those sites began leaking waste again less than a year after the EPA pronounced it safe. By 1990, cleanup operations had been completed at fewer than 100 sites. Despite its shortcomings, however, Superfund remains the nation's number-one weapon against chemical hazards that already exist. In 1986 Congress expanded Superfund with an additional $8.5 billion and also passed the Right-to-Know Act, which gives citizens access to information about chemical processing and storage in their communities.

Will more Love Canals bubble to the surface in the coming years? Almost certainly. With perhaps half a million hazardous waste sites scattered around the country, ranging from enormous manufacturing plants to abandoned, half-empty, leaking underground gas tanks, it is unlikely that the United States can escape further outbreaks of chemical poisoning. Many other nations face the same unpleasant prospect. On the positive side,

*Czechoslovak president Vaclav Havel visits the toxic waste dump in the village of Chabarovice, one of the largest and most dangerous waste dumps in all of Europe.*

however, the problem has been recognized. The worst sites are being cleaned up, however slowly and uncertainly. Laws are in place that if strictly enforced can keep new toxic time bombs from being set ticking.

Most important, perhaps, is the growing public awareness of the toxic problem. A few decades ago, only dedicated environmentalists worried about such issues as toxic wastes. But in 1992 a national survey by *Parade* magazine found that 68% of Americans claimed to be "very concerned" about the buildup of waste materials, and 83% favored more government regulation of industrial waste. Some concerned members of the public have rolled up their sleeves and tackled the problem directly. A South Carolina homemaker named Carol Boykin, for example, helped found Citizens Asking for a Safe Environment (CASE), a local organization that protested against a hazardous waste dump situated on top of a groundwater aquifer. CASE mustered 7,000 members in four years and forced the dump to close. It also brought before the state legislature a bill that could eventually ban all hazardous waste disposal in South Carolina.

Local grass-roots organizations have brought about change, closings, and cleanups in many communities. These groups—called NIMBYs for their slogan, "Not In My Back Yard"—are often regarded as pests by the chemical industry and even by the EPA and local governments. Yet they may be the single most powerful force working against further toxic chemical disasters.

*In Prince William Sound in Alaska, the Exxon* Baton Rouge *comes alongside the crippled Exxon* Valdez *to off-load the supertanker's remaining unspilled oil.*

chapter 4


# OIL SPILLS


Roughly one-quarter of the oil pumped in the United States comes from wells in or near Prudhoe Bay, on Alaska's north shore. It flows south across the length of Alaska through the trans-Alaska pipeline, sometimes at the rate of more than 2 million barrels a day. When it reaches the southern end of the pipeline at the port city of Valdez, it is loaded into super-tankers—ships that carry it on the next leg of its southbound trip toward the refineries that will turn it into fuel. The tankers pass through Prince William Sound, one of the most majestic meeting places of sea and rugged land in a state that is famous for its spectacular, unspoiled beauty.

Early in the morning of March 24, 1987, a tanker loaded with 53 million gallons of Alaska crude oil was moving south through the sound. It was the Exxon *Valdez,* owned by the Exxon Shipping Company, a division of the multinational oil company. The ship's captain, Joseph Hazelwood, ordered a course change, moving the ship out of the prescribed southbound shipping lane in order to avoid icebergs. He then left the ship's bridge, or control center, instructing the third mate to return to the regular shipping lane a few minutes later. But the *Valdez* never corrected its course. Eleven minutes after Hazelwood left the bridge, the ship ran aground on the Bligh Reef, a mass of granite pinnacles near Bligh Island on the eastern side of the sound.

The force of the impact drove masses of rock up through the tanker's hull and ripped open eight of its oil tanks. Unable to break free, the *Valdez* perched precariously on the reef, bleeding oil into the sound, while its captain radioed the bad news to the Coast Guard. Over the next couple of days, news broadcasts carried the ominous message of an oil spill to audiences around the country and around the world. People were saddened and angered by images of otters, eagles, and seabirds struggling help-lessly against the sticky black tide that had invaded their world.

The *Valdez* disaster was not the first or the worst oil spill the world had seen. The term *oil spill* came into common use as early as 1967, when a tanker called the *Torrey Canyon* sank near the Scilly Isles off the southwest coast of Britain. In the world's first large-scale spill, the *Torrey Canyon* emptied 37 million gallons of oil into the sea, which later washed it up on beaches. In 1978 the *Amoco Cadiz* spilled 68 million gallons on the coast of France; the French shoreline was badly polluted as a result.

As the world's demand for oil continued to increase, the drilling and shipping of oil necessarily increased as well. And increased traffic meant increased risk of accidents. Two serious spills occurred in 1979. Near the island of Trinidad in the south-ern Caribbean, the *Atlantic Empress* collided with the *Aegean Captain;* 110 million gallons of oil were spilled. And an explosion at *Ixtoc 1,* an oil well in Campeche Bay off the Yucatán Peninsula of Mexico, created one of the biggest spills of all time: 200 million gallons. A year later the *Irene's Serenade* sank in Greek waters, spilling 35 million gallons of oil.

The litany of disasters continued. One of the worst spills occurred in 1983, when an offshore oil rig collapsed in the Persian Gulf, releasing 220 million gallons of oil into the water. In that same year the *Castillo del Beliver* caught fire at the Cape of Good Hope in South Africa, spilling 75 million gallons of oil and polluting the shore with soot.

Some people hoped that although the world's offshore oil fields and busy shipping lanes might suffer, its more remote wilderness waters would remain untouched by the blights of civilization. But early in 1989 an Argentine freighter spilled 170,000 gallons of diesel fuel in Antarctic waters, causing Antarctica's first major oil spill. Then in March came the *Valdez* disaster. In April a tanker ran aground in the Red Sea, spilling 1 million gallons of oil on coral reefs. Later in 1989, three separate incidents in American waters totaled 1.5 million gallons spilled. In 1990 an Iranian supertanker called the *Kharg-5* exploded off the coast of Morocco, spilling 20 million gallons of oil.

The year 1993 began with two big spills on opposite sides of the earth. In January the *Braer,* a tanker carrying oil from Norway to Canada, took a shortcut to save time and ended up breaking apart in a rocky bay in the Shetland Islands, 200 miles north of Scotland. Nearly 25 million gallons of oil spilled into the bay. Oil washed ashore on beaches, spread through prime fish habitats, shut down salmon fisheries, and killed birds, seals, and otters. In an unusual touch, the oil was also lifted into the air by the Shetlands' powerful winds. It was carried inshore to contaminate acres of the grassland from which many of the sheep-rearing islanders make their living.

Several weeks later, two ships collided in the Bay of Bengal, east of India. They were near the entrance to one of the

*In Prince William Sound, a cleanup crew sprays seawater over the rocky shore to wash oil from the crippled Exxon Valdez back into the ocean, where it can be contained by skimmers.*

world's busiest waterways, the Strait of Malacca, a sea channel that separates Indonesia from the Asian mainland. The strait is part of the standard route for many ships traveling between the Indian Ocean and eastern Asia. One of the ships was an empty tanker. The other, a Danish vessel called the *Maersk Navigator,* was carrying 84 million gallons of oil from Oman to Japan. It caught on fire and burned for six days. Thirty thousand tons of oil spilled, creating three large slicks, or patches of oil floating on the ocean's surface, that drifted through fragile marine habitats, threatening the survival not just of fish but also of rare turtles and dugongs, large marine mammals similar to the manatees native to Florida waters.

To many people, the words *oil spill* conjure up pathetic pictures of dead and dying birds and animals, struggling vainly on befouled shores. Certainly the immediate deaths of wildlife and the pollution of seacoasts are the most obvious results of oil spills. But the long-term effects of the spills are not well understood, nor do scientists and spill-management experts know how best to control spills and limit the harm they do. The *Valdez* spill, tragically unnecessary though it was, has served as a laboratory in which scientists can study the effects of oil pollution and experiment with new cleanup methods. It has also served as a costly lesson in the pitfalls of petroleum shipping and the shortcomings of emergency plans.

Many of the scientists and oil industry experts who have worked at the site of the *Valdez* disaster cannot yet discuss their findings because those findings are evidence in the court battles that will probably go on for years as Exxon, the state of Alaska, and hundreds of citizens wrangle over responsibility and compensation for the spill. But the outline of events after the tanker ran aground is fairly clear.

There was a significant delay in getting workers and emergency equipment to the site of the spill and organizing the emergency team. Since the 1970s, when Congress approved the building of the Alaskan pipeline, plans had existed for dealing with a spill in Alaskan waters. Pipeline operators, oil companies, and state and federal officials were supposed to know what to do, and they were supposed to have the necessary equipment ready at all times. But when disaster struck, it took the Alyeska Pipeline Service Company's response team 12 hours to cover the 28 miles to the spill site instead of the 5 hours their contract demanded. Furthermore, their equipment was sufficient only for a spill of 1,000 to 2,000 barrels, while the *Valdez* spill was many times larger (a barrel of oil is equal to 42 gallons). Alyeska officials had reportedly claimed that a large spill could happen only once in 241 years. When he heard this, a member of a local fisherman's union replied, "There's a saying that only one in a hundred Alaska brown bears will bite. Trouble is, they don't come in numerical order."

Coast Guard and Exxon crews began working to empty the wounded tanker so that its remaining 42 million gallons would not be added to the spill. They also tried to skim the spilled oil from the surface of the water. But due to lack of experience with the equipment and the absence of a barge into which to pump the skimmed oil, the skimming was not very effective, although the *Valdez* was emptied without further leakage.

A basic tactic in responding to spills is to contain them, or keep them from spreading, with floating barriers called booms. Soon after the spill, local fishermen grabbed all available booms and tried to protect the herring and salmon hatcheries in the sound, but they were able to contain only a tiny fraction of the oil. Exxon later chartered military transport planes and flew large booms from all over the world to the sound, but the containment effort was a case of too little, too late. The extremely cold temperature of the water had caused the oil to thicken, which made it hard to collect. However, the booms were later very useful in the cleanup campaign.

Weather conditions also determined the effectiveness of another form of emergency response: the use of dispersants, or chemical agents similar to detergents, that break up oil and allow it to mix with water. Heavy wave action is needed to mix the dispersants with the oil, but the sound remained calm for several days after the accident, and the federal official in charge on the scene decided that dispersants would do no good. By the time tests had proved that dispersants *would* be effective, a high wind sprang up, making it impossible to spray the dispersants. At any rate, Exxon had not obtained enough dispersants to do the job. In short, efforts to contain or neutralize the spill right after it happened were largely unsuccessful. The plume of oil spread out and continued to move down the sound, which is dotted with many islands.

Prince William Sound was only the beginning. Within a couple of months, the oil had traveled hundreds of miles along

*Boats in Prince William Sound use special booms to contain the oil spilled by the Exxon Valdez.*

the Gulf of Alaska, tainting shorelines on the Kenai Peninsula, the Alaska Peninsula, and scores of islands, including Kodiak Island. Four national wildlife refuges, three national parks, and the Chugach National Forest were hit. In all, the spill fouled 1,200 miles of coastline—equal to the distance between Boston and the Outer Banks of North Carolina.

The dangers of petroleum to wildlife are well established. Seabirds can become too heavily coated with oil to fly; when they try to clean the oil from their feathers with their beaks, it poisons them. Even birds that do not die at once are at risk, because small amounts of petroleum taken into their systems can cause anemia. Sea otters and seals contaminated with oil may be blinded or suffer injury to the lungs, liver, and kidneys; these conditions are often fatal. In addition, the otters' fur loses its ability to insulate them when it is coated with oil, and they can die of hypothermia, or exposure to cold. Animals such as eagles, bears, wolverines, and foxes that scavenge meals from oil-soaked carcasses washed up on shore are themselves contaminated. And fish can be damaged directly by the oil, or indirectly by its effects on the plants and microorganisms that make up their food chain. The spill's exact death toll will never be known, but at least 1,000 sea otters and 100,000 birds (including 150 bald eagles) were killed.

Fortunately, the bulk of the oil did not sink to the sea bottom, where it might have exerted a long-term effect on basic ecological processes. Instead, most of it ultimately washed ashore. There cleanup crews toiled for months, experimenting with a variety of techniques to remove the thick, tarry oil from rocky beaches and coves.

Workers—as many as 11,000 of them—converged on the stricken shoreline. Some were environmentalists; others were ordinary people from a number of states who received an hourly wage for their efforts. But many were volunteers who felt a need to do something, anything, to help. Some worked at animal rescue centers, cleaning birds and administering medical care to stricken sea otters. Local residents used household utensils to scoop oil from shallow water, or scoured beach boulders with paper towels. Critics pointed out that such "rock-scrubbing" was often futile, because the waves soon washed more oil ashore. But workers clung to the belief that "every little bit helps," as one high-school student said while blotting oil from a stretch of beach with old clothes.

More sophisticated methods were also used in the cleanup. Teams surrounded contaminated areas with booms and then used high-pressure hoses on the beaches to loosen the oil, which was collected with absorbent polyester mops or driven offshore to be gathered by skimmers. In an experimental program called bioremediation, scientists sprayed specially blended fertilizers on contaminated beaches. These fertilizers stimulated the growth of naturally occurring bacteria that break down and consume oil. The process was surprisingly effective and will probably be used on other spills, although biologists warn that the fertilizers themselves may have a destructive effect on the marine environment if they are overused.

Will Prince William Sound and the Gulf of Alaska recover? Experts have argued on both sides of the question, but it is too soon to be sure one way or the other. Scientists who have monitored the fate of other spill sites, such as the French beaches

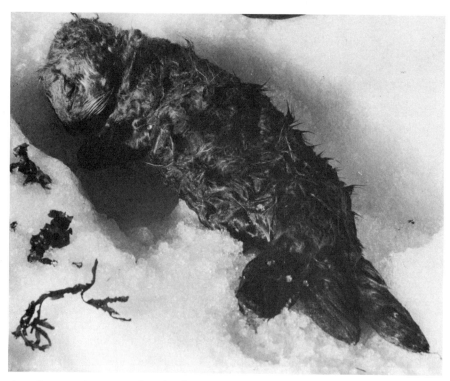

An oil-covered sea otter lies dead on an ice-covered beach in Prince William Sound after the Exxon *Valdez* oil spill.

that were contaminated by the *Amoco Cadiz* in 1978, have learned that nature has remarkable powers of recovery—yet they also caution that the resilience of natural ecosystems does not mean that they can be taken for granted or carelessly abused.

A year after the *Valdez* spill, some biologists working at the site were cautiously optimistic. Although area fishermen had lost millions of dollars in income in the 1989–90 season, fish populations did not appear to have suffered an irreversible decline. The oil content of water and sediment samples was lower than some experts had expected. Yet fish and shellfish from the waters affected by the spill must be tested for contamination, and many samples have proven unsafe to eat because their flesh contains high concentrations of compounds found in petroleum.

Only one thing about the aftermath of the *Valdez* spill is certain, and that is that lawsuits will drag their way through the courts for years to come. In July 1992 the Alaska Court of Appeals overturned a criminal conviction against Joseph Hazelwood, the captain of the *Valdez*, who had been accused of negligence and intoxication. The state attorney general plans to appeal this ruling in the Alaska Supreme Court, hoping for a criminal conviction. Exxon fired Hazelwood; the Coast Guard suspended his license for less than a year. During the three years after the spill, Exxon spent $2.5 billion on cleanup efforts and promised $1 billion more. But some Alaskans claim that this is not enough to rehabilitate the injured region. Exxon and Hazelwood still face an array of civil lawsuits filed by Alaskan citizens, businesses, and environmental groups.

In the midst of recriminations and lawsuits, the U.S. Congress, the oil industry, and a host of environmental groups have begun discussing new laws that would require stricter control of tanker operations and better training for emergency crews. One proposal from the oil industry calls for a $250 million program to set up five regional emergency response centers, each equipped to handle a spill of 8.4 million gallons. Another possibility is to require tankers to have double hulls, which might prevent them from rupturing in the event of an accident. Scientists are also analyzing the results of cleanup programs in Alaska and working to develop new and more efficient methods of containing and removing spilled oil.

Behind these efforts lies an inescapable reality: it will happen again. As long as the world's dependence upon fossil fuels continues to grow, oil will be drilled and shipped, and spills will occur. But spills from accidents account for only part of the oil that pollutes the world's waters. For every thousand tons of oil shipped, a ton is emptied into the sea in the course of routine operations such as rinsing out tanks with seawater. *The Global Ecology Handbook,* a 1990 publication, reports that two-thirds of all oceanic oil pollution is caused by the everyday activities of the petroleum shipping industry, and only one-third is caused by spills. Those who want to see oil pollution reduced point out that we will need to do more than develop better emergency procedures: we will need to revise the way oil is routinely handled. Better yet would be to develop alternative sources of energy and reduce our use of oil.

*After the Exxon* Valdez *oil spill in Prince William Sound, Alaska, in 1989, fish hatcheries pump baby salmon from the sea into special holding tanks to protect them from the oil slick.*

One legacy of the *Valdez* disaster that offers hope for the future is the Valdez Principles, drawn up in September 1989 by a cluster of environmental groups and investment businesses, including the Sierra Club, the National Audubon Society, and the Social Investment Forum. Named after the Alaskan spill, the Valdez Principles are a set of guidelines for environmentally responsible investment and development. Companies that subscribe to the Valdez code of conduct agree to reduce pollution, strive for more efficient use of energy, and take responsibility for repairing damage to the environment. Consumers and investors who want their dollars to go to companies that help, rather than hurt, the environment can find out whether those companies have pledged to support the Valdez Principles. The code's founders also urge college students who are planning their careers to consider a company's commitment to environmental responsibility when they are thinking of taking a job. Only if enough individuals show that protecting the environment is important to them will corporations and governments change course and steer away from oil—and from the certainty of future oil spills.

The exhaust towers of the Three Mile Island nuclear reactor near Harrisburg, Pennsylvania.

# chapter 5

# NUCLEAR COUNTDOWN

One of the defining events of the 20th century occurred in 1945, during World War II, when the United States dropped atomic bombs on Japan. They were the first—and, so far, the only—nuclear weapons ever launched in war. The devastation they wrought on the Japanese cities of Hiroshima and Nagasaki brought the war to an end and impressed the world with the titanic power of the new force that had been unleashed.

In the decades following the war, nuclear power seemed to have two faces, one evil and the other good. The dark side of nuclear power was foremost in many minds in the aftermath of Hiroshima. No weapon had ever dealt death and destruction on so large a scale, and people were afraid it would happen again. These fears grew to fever pitch at times during the Cold War, a decades-long period of mutual distrust and hostility between the United States and its allies, and the communist powers led by the Soviet Union.

As both sides stockpiled nuclear weapons, ordinary people wondered what would happen if war broke out. Individuals and government agencies built fallout shelters—underground retreats designed to protect people from lethal radioactive particles that fall from the sky after nuclear explosions—even though some experts predicted that such shelters would not offer much real protection from the horrors of all-out nuclear war. In the 1960s and 1970s, people made uneasy references to the "panic button" and worried that doomsday might come about because a nervous soldier overreacted to a malfunction on a radar screen. In the 1980s, when nuclear weapons had become numerous and were far more powerful than the bombs dropped on Japan, scientists began talking about nuclear winter, a period of prolonged darkness and cold that might be caused by a nuclear war. It was predicted that nuclear winter would mean the end of civilization, perhaps even of life on earth.

But there was also a positive side to nuclear power. In the 1950s, nuclear power was promoted as a new source of energy, one that would transform the world with almost limitless supplies of electricity. Nuclear engineers—many of them graduates of weapons development programs—turned their attention to designing and building nuclear power plants. They claimed that nuclear energy would be clean, cheap, and safe. Critics of the nuclear industry say that they were wrong on all three counts.

By the late 1980s, fears of nuclear war had to some extent subsided. Although peace is fragile and cannot be taken for granted, a series of disarmament treaties among the superpowers and the end of the Cold War have caused the prospect of nuclear war to recede a bit. Ironically, however, it is the "good" side of nuclear power that now worries people. Nuclear power plants, which once seemed to be the answer to the ever-growing need for energy, are now seen as potent health threats. Some scientists, physicians, and environmentalists believe that the world's nuclear power plants are more dangerous than its nuclear warheads.

## RADIOACTIVITY

Nuclear energy, whether in a power plant or in a bomb, is produced by radiation, or changes inside atoms that cause energy to be emitted in the form of extremely tiny fast-moving particles. Some naturally occurring elements, such as uranium, are radioactive. But high-energy radiation—radiation powerful enough to operate a steam turbine or damage living cells—must be created. This is done through fission, a reaction in which the nucleus of an atom is split, giving off a burst of energy. Nuclear power plants contain large chambers called reactors; inside the reactors, nuclear fission reactions are created and maintained using radioactive material as fuel for the reaction. Although there are various ways of harnessing the energy given off by the reaction, in most power plants the fission reaction heats water, creating steam that is used to operate turbines.

Some reactors are called breeder reactors—they produce more radioactive material, in the form of highly radioactive plutonium, than they use. These are the reactors that manufacture plutonium for nuclear warheads. In the United States, breeder reactors are operated by the Department of Energy (DOE) and controlled by the government. But ordinary commercial reactors are owned and operated by local utility companies, under the supervision of a government-appointed board called the Nuclear Regulatory Commission (NRC).

One characteristic of radioactivity is its longevity. Every radioactive substance has what scientists call a half-life; this is the time it will take for one-half of the radioactive atoms in the substance to disintegrate naturally. Uranium-238, for example, has a half-life of 4.5 billion years. This means that it will take 4.5

*A photograph of the nuclear power plant at Chernobyl, near Kiev in the Ukraine, taken before what may be the worst nuclear accident in history.*

billion years for a bar of uranium to give off half its radio-activity, and another 4.5 billion years for it to give off half of what remains, and so on. Many radioactive materials can continue to emit dangerous levels of radiation for thousands of years.

Radiation is dangerous to all forms of life. Decades before the first man-made fission reaction, workers in watch factories experienced unusually high rates of illness, particularly cancers of the mouth and throat. It turned out that the sick workers were those who painted glow-in-the-dark numerals on the watch faces, using paint that contained small amounts of radium, a naturally occurring radioactive substance. They were in the habit of licking their brushes to bring them to a sharp point, and over the years they had ingested enough radium to make them ill.

At very high intensities, radiation can kill instantly. Its effects are similar to those of fire—bodies of radiation victims, such as those in Hiroshima and Nagasaki, are often blackened and distorted. Even when exposure to radiation is not immediately fatal, victims suffer severe burning and blistering. But the real damage is hidden. Radiation penetrates living cells and destroys them, which can cause cancer to develop years after the exposure. One form of radiation with which everyone is familiar is sunlight. Exposure to sunlight can burn the skin and cause skin cancer. Exposure to more intense radiation, such as that given off by reactor fuel, has been linked to cancer of the lungs, stomach, bowels, liver, blood cells, and other parts of the body. It also damages genetic material, causing birth defects.

Radiation in the air, water, or soil is measured in units called curies, named after Marie and Pierre Curie, the discoverers of radium. In terms of human health, exposure to radiation is usually measured in units called rems and millirems (a millirem is one-thousandth of a rem). A person exposed to 600 rems will generally die within 60 days; half of all people exposed to 400 rems will die. At the other end of the spectrum, most Americans absorb an average of about 100 millirems each year, from cosmic radiation, X rays, and the background radiation of nuclear activities such as bomb tests. It is the middle range of exposure that is troubling. Scientists are still trying to determine exactly how moderate radiation exposure is related to disease and genetic damage.

# EXPLOSION AT CHERNOBYL

When arguing that nuclear plants are dangerous, opponents of nuclear power have only to point to Chernobyl, the site of the worst reported nuclear accident in history.

Chernobyl is a town in the Ukraine, formerly part of the Soviet Union. There the Soviets built a complex of four nuclear reactors, each of which produced enough electricity to light a city the size of Toledo, Ohio. Chernobyl was regarded as a reliable, safe facility—until April 25, 1986. On that date engineers at Chernobyl's reactor 4 began preparing to test certain procedures. In doing so, they broke a number of their own safety rules. They turned off an emergency cooling system, and they withdrew the rods that controlled the intensity of the reaction.

By early the following morning the computer showed that excessive radiation was being produced inside the reactor, but the engineers overrode the automatic shutdown signals and began the test with manual adjustments of the control rods. This was, said a Soviet expert later, like "airplane pilots experimenting with the engines in flight." The reaction had become dangerously unstable, and suddenly it went out of control. Within four seconds the power had surged to more than 100 times the reactor's limits. A large amount of uranium disintegrated and burst through the graphite blocks that surrounded it. When it hit the water that was used to cool the reactor, this superheated uranium and graphite caused a massive explosion of steam, blowing the top off the reactor. Chunks of burning uranium and graphite rose into the air and showered down, while a three-mile-high plume of radioactive dust and soot rose into the atmosphere.

The Soviet government quickly dropped a veil of secrecy over the Chernobyl disaster—the government did not publicly acknowledge that the explosion had occurred until April 28, two days later. By then, however, radiation detectors in Sweden and elsewhere had picked up the first signs of radioactive fallout. The radioactive plume that had risen from Chernobyl divided into two streams; one of them drifted across Europe, the other across Asia to the Pacific and eventually to Alaska. The worst airborne contamination fell inside the Soviet Union and in Europe.

Across Europe, people reacted in fear and outrage. Radiation testing kits were distributed, and people got used to checking the air and water for contamination. Radio and newspaper announcements advised people to wash their clothes daily and rinse their shoes before entering their homes to avoid carrying contaminated dust into their living quarters. Millions of dollars' worth of agricultural produce—Italian wheat, German

*These two children, being treated for radiation-related illnesses at a Minsk Hospital, were underneath the radioactive cloud that spread over Russia after the explosion at Chernobyl.*

powdered milk, Polish potatoes, Dutch butter, English lamb—
were found to be contaminated and were destroyed. Among the
hardest hit were the Lapps, a nomadic reindeer-herding people
of northern Scandinavia and northeastern Russia. Radioactive
contamination was especially heavy in that region, and whole
herds of reindeer had to be destroyed, dealing a heavy blow to
the Lapps' economy and traditional way of life.

Damage to food supplies was bad, but the specter of
radiation sickness also had to be faced. Although scientists think
that most people in Europe received less than 10 millirems of
radiation exposure, people in Scandinavia and the western Soviet
Union almost certainly received higher doses. No one knows
what long-term effect this will have on their health. In the
Ukraine, close to the explosion, contamination was much
more severe.

It is impossible to say what the ultimate death toll of
Chernobyl will be. Thirty-one Soviets died in the accident or soon
after it from injuries or radiation sickness. More than 116,000
people were evacuated from the area within an 18-mile radius of
the reactor. Of these, 24,500 received high doses of radiation;
scientists estimate that 100 to 200 of them will get cancer
because of the accident. Estimates of the Chernobyl-caused fatal
illnesses that will arise in Europe and the former Soviet Union
over the coming years range from 5,000 to 75,000.

The explosion was financially costly as well. The
evacuated residents needed medical care and new housing, but
the biggest cost has been cleaning up the radioactive debris. The
Soviets acted quickly to bury the debris in lead, sand, and clay.
Then they entombed the whole reactor in a giant cage of steel

and concrete, which is surrounded by barriers and sensing devices. The experts who designed this casing hope that it will remain secure and leak free for a long time, for it will be hundreds of years before the radioactive material inside the structure decays enough to allow humans to enter it. They do not know, however, if the protective shielding they have built will do the job. The Chernobyl containment is the first of its kind, but outside observers studying the containment structure in the 1990s have concluded that it is already deteriorating.

Chernobyl was the worst nuclear accident known, but there have been others. Two serious incidents occurred in 1957, early in the nuclear age. At the Windscale nuclear plant in Britain, a reactor fire released a large amount of radioactive polonium and iodine into the environment; several hundred cases of cancers are believed to have been caused by this contamination. And an accident at a nuclear weapons plant near Kyshtym, in Russia's Ural Mountains, caused hundreds of deaths and required the evacuation of 10,000 people; because of policies of secrecy, however, the Soviet Union did not admit that the Kyshtym incident had occurred until 30 years later.

The United States, too, has had a serious nuclear accident. On March 28, 1979, mechanical flaws combined with operator errors caused a near tragedy at a reactor at the Three Mile Island (TMI) nuclear plant in Pennsylvania. The reactor came very close to a state called meltdown, in which the reactor's casing is melted by high heat, and large amounts of radiation are released. Some radioactive contamination did leak from the reactor core into the environment, but nearly all of the contamination was captured within the plant. No one died as a

*A Russian soldier prepares a grave at a memorial ceremony for the firemen and rescue workers who died trying to contain the release of radiation at the Chernobyl reactor.*

direct result of the leak, but some experts are concerned that people who were in the area at the time might be at increased risk for disease later in life.

The TMI reactor was shut down immediately, and the task of cleaning up the damage and dismantling the reactor began. The cleanup has been a long, costly nightmare. At first, power company officials said that it would take two years and $140 million to dismantle the reactor and clean up the radioactive debris. In 1993, 14 years after the accident, the cleanup was still going on, and more than $1 billion had been spent. Yet more radioactive debris remains to be disposed of, and no one has been able to determine what should be done with the severely contaminated reactor shell itself. It could be taken apart and removed to a storage facility, or it could be encased in a protective tomb like that at Chernobyl. Current estimates say that the TMI cleanup cannot be finished until 2014. Taxpayers and electric rate payers will pay the rising costs of the cleanup—and they are still footing the bill for building the reactor in the first place.

## NUCLEAR ISSUES TODAY

In the years following the near meltdown at TMI, nuclear industry officials and environmentalists took a close look at nuclear practices in the United States. They found that accidents and mishaps are disturbingly common in nuclear facilities. In the 10 years after the TMI accident there were 33,000 reported mishaps, emergency shutdowns, leaks or discharges of radioactive water or gas, or other potentially dangerous incidents at the nation's power plants. A thousand of these incidents were serious, although none approached the severity of TMI. Some of them involved radioactive discharges that were not reported to the public.

About three-quarters of all accidents were caused by workers making mistakes or failing to do their jobs properly. At Pennsylvania's Peach Bottom reactor number 3, for example, senior operators were found sleeping and playing video games in the control room. When the NRC discovered in 1986 that many reactor operators were failing safety examinations, a committee appointed by Congress recommended that the problem could be solved by eliminating the tests because operators became depressed when they failed to pass them. Instead, the NRC developed new tests, but the testing program is not always carried out in full.

Other reactor incidents were caused by mechanical failures: leaks in pipes, electrical short circuits, and the like. Such failures are sometimes overlooked in the interest of continuing to provide electricity to consumers. At TMI, for instance, the power company and NRC inspectors knew of a leak in reactor number 2 six months before the accident, but the inspectors allowed the power company to continue operating the reactor instead of shutting it down. The NRC and the power company kept this fact secret from the public.

The list of nuclear near-miss disasters adds up to a grim total. Some people who have studied the nuclear industry worry that another major disaster could occur at any time. James Asseltine, who served on the Nuclear Regulatory Commission during the 1980s, was one of the few commissioners who have frankly criticized the nuclear industry. In 1986 he claimed that the United States had a 45% chance of undergoing a serious nuclear accident within 20 years.

Accidents are not the only problem with nuclear plants. Equally pressing is the question of what to do with nuclear waste. Radioactive material is produced as a byproduct of mining uranium and also of operating fission reactions. All radioactive substances are dangerous, but some wastes are highly radioactive and extremely toxic. Because of their long half-life they will remain deadly for hundreds or thousands of years. Where and how should these deadly wastes be stored?

When the boom in building nuclear power plants began, no one gave any thought to the disposal of radioactive wastes. But as the wastes began to pile up, their safe disposal became a matter of some urgency. Physicians for Social Responsibility, an antinuclear organization, calls the buildup of nuclear waste a "creeping Chernobyl," with tremendous destructive potential. Radioactive waste has been dumped into the sea and into landfills. It has leaked into groundwater sources and drinking wells. But a great deal of nuclear waste, including most of the highest-level waste—intensely radioactive uranium and plutonium fuel rods—is sitting around in tanks and cooling ponds at nuclear plants, waiting for proper storage facilities to be available.

Two such facilities are planned by the federal government, which in 1982 passed the Nuclear Waste Policy Act to regulate the handling of nuclear waste. The act authorizes the creation of an underground chamber for storing low-level radioactive waste in Carlsbad, New Mexico, and one for high-level waste at Yucca Mountain, Nevada. The Carlsbad site

*Americans demonstrate against the dangers of nuclear power.*

has encountered problems both from New Mexicans who are opposed to it and from structural flaws, such as cracks in the underground walls; it will probably not open until sometime in the early 21st century, if ever. The Yucca Mountain site, which is located on traditional lands of the Shoshone Native American people, may prove to be unsuitable because of the danger of underground flooding or earthquakes that could release the contaminants into the water or air. Officials in Nevada have rejected the plan, and the facility will almost certainly not be available by the target date of 2010. In the meantime, temporary storage facilities are filling up, and the problem of what to do with the waste becomes ever more complicated and costly. A study cited in the *Washington Post* in 1988 reported that of every dollar the DOE spends on developing nuclear weapons, 45 cents must be spent on waste management.

In the eyes of many environmentalists, the Department of Energy and its nuclear weapons facilities are worse offenders than the commercially operated power plants. DOE facilities are not monitored by the NRC; for years they operated without public scrutiny. Yet their operations have sometimes been monumentally unsafe. One of the most notorious DOE sites is at Hanford, Washington, on the banks of the Columbia River. In 1956, nearly half a million gallons of highly radioactive water were spilled there and seeped into nearby groundwater sources, which have been found to be severely contaminated. During the 1940s and 1950s, smokestacks at Hanford leaked large amounts of radioactive contamination into the air. On one occasion the plant's engineers deliberately released a plume of radioactive iodine gas as part of an experiment. Fallout from the plume landed on a 8,000-square-mile area of Washington and Oregon.

But although this leak contained more than 200 times as much radioactivity as the leak from Three Mile Island, the public was not informed that it had taken place.

Hanford, where tons of radioactive waste are stored, is regarded as the most contaminated and potentially dangerous nuclear site in the United States. It and three other unsafe DOE sites—Fernald, Ohio; the Savannah River in South Carolina; and Rocky Flats, Colorado—were shut down by the government in the late 1980s. Experts estimate that it will cost billions of dollars to decontaminate these sites and move their wastes to a permanent storage facility—if one ever becomes available.

Nuclear warheads, submarines, and satellites also pose the risk of environmental disaster. In 1963 the U.S. nuclear submarine *Thresher* sank off the coast of Massachusetts; two years later the U.S. aircraft carrier *Ticonderoga* lost a nuclear warhead in the sea near Japan. In 1973 a nuclear submarine leaked radioactive coolant into Puget Sound in the Pacific Northwest. These are not isolated incidents: in 1989 the environmental group Greenpeace reported on a study that showed that the navies of the world had experienced as many as 1,200 nuclear mishaps and had left 50 warheads and 9 reactors lying on the seabed. No one knows what long-term effects these may produce. That same year, there were three more nuclear accidents at sea, involving two Soviet nuclear submarines and an American ship.

A nuclear accident could also happen in space. What goes up sometimes comes down—unexpectedly. The Soviet *Cosmos 954* satellite spilled radioactive debris over a 40,000-square-mile area of Canada in 1978. A decade later California congressman George E. Brown, Jr., introduced a bill into Congress that would ban nuclear reactors in space. "A major catastrophe has been avoided in large part because only a few percent of today's spacecraft have a nuclear power source on board," he said. "But there could well be hundreds of nuclear reactors circling the earth in the 21st century. How lucky will we be then?" The bill did not pass. At the time there were approximately 50 nuclear-powered satellites in earth's orbit; more have since been launched.

Back at the dawn of the nuclear age, in the heyday of reactor building, no one gave much thought to what would happen when nuclear power plants outlived their usefulness. Today, however, power plants in the United States and elsewhere are growing old and shutting down well ahead of schedule. Although reactors were expected to last for about 40 years, many of the parts used in them were warrantied for much shorter periods of time, perhaps 15 years or less. As tubes crack, pipes corrode, and other symptoms of decay set in, many utility companies are finding that repairs would be too expensive. A number of reactors have therefore been decommissioned, or taken out of use, much earlier than had been planned.

In early 1993 the Trojan reactor in Oregon was shut down, 18 years ahead of schedule, because it would have cost more than $200 million to repair. But the people of Oregon now face as much as $500 million in expenses for decommissioning the reactor: dismantling it, storing its radioactive waste, and so on. The decommissioning of Trojan left 109 commercial reactors in operation in the United States, and as many as 25 of them were expected to be shut down by the year 2000. In 1989, the international Atomic Energy Agency predicted that at least 71 of the 430 reactors operating in 25 countries around the world would be out of service by the year 2000.

*At a naval base in Norfolk, Virginia, a nuclear-powered aircraft carrier awaits refitting. Many people have questioned the wisdom of keeping nuclear-powered and nuclear-armed naval vessels docked near large cities.*

Nuclear industry promoters had expected that new reactors would be built as old ones died. But the boom in reactor building appears to have ended. The last new application for a reactor license in the United States was granted in 1978; plants that are now under construction are being built on licenses granted before that year. Nuclear development is slowing down in some other countries as well. Sweden and Germany have voted to limit or phase out nuclear power. A reactor accident in Japan in 1991 may have slowed that country's plans for rapid nuclear development. In France, however, a strong plan of nuclear development continues to be supported by the government and most citizens; 75% of France's electricity is generated by nuclear power.

Activism by concerned citizens is one of the forces that has slowed nuclear development. The NIMBY syndrome—Not in My Back Yard—has caught on around the world. In Germany the Green party, whose political platform emphasizes environmental caretaking, has successfully opposed nuclear building plans. In the Ukraine and the other republics of the former Soviet Union, where activism was officially repressed for decades, the legacy of Chernobyl has turned many people into activists. A Ukrainian physician named Yuri Shcherbak started the Green World environmental movement after Chernobyl; later he became the Ukraine's minister of the environment. A citizens' group in Kazakhstan, a former Soviet republic that is now an independent state, won a NIMBY victory when it shut down a nuclear testing range that had caused hundreds, perhaps thousands, of illnesses and deaths from radioactivity.

In the United States, too, local activists have won some major battles against nuclear development. In 1989 voters shut down the Rancho Seco plant in California. The Shoreham plant in Long Island, New York, built between 1973 and 1984 at a cost of $5.5 billion, was never put into service because opponents of the plant blocked its use. Activists have also delayed or postponed the building or start-up of other facilities. But the key reason that nuclear development has slowed almost to a halt is economics. Promoters of nuclear energy claimed that it would be cheaper than oil or coal, but it has proven to be more expensive. Worker training, safety precautions, public relations, legal fees—every aspect of operating a nuclear plant has been about 10 times more costly than was originally estimated. Many utility companies have lost money or gone bankrupt after spending large amounts on nuclear plants. I. C. Bupp, a Massachusetts energy consultant, stated in January 1993, "There is no market in the utility industry for nuclear power."

Yet is the nuclear age really over? Some industry experts predict that nuclear power will make a comeback. They point out that the public is now worried about global warming and greenhouse gases—and that nuclear power does not produce greenhouse gases or contribute to global warming as the burning of fossil fuels does. Companies such as General Electric and Westinghouse are pushing a new generation of what they call idiot-proof reactors, with improved safety features. Even some environmentalists are beginning to agree that nuclear power may be preferable to the continued burning of oil, coal, and the world's last remaining forests.

As long as humanity's appetite for energy continues to grow, it is unlikely that nuclear power can be altogether dismissed. But the troubling questions remain: How can we prevent another Chernobyl or Three Mile Island? And what will we do with the dangerous waste that nuclear power creates?

*During the Vietnam War, U.S. aircraft prepare to spray defoliants near the Vietnam-Cambodian border. These chemicals not only cleared away the forests but also caused health problems for the servicemen doing the spraying.*

chapter    6


# T H E   S P O I L S   O F   W A R


The phrase *spoils of war* usually refers to prizes or wealth gained through combat: perhaps the land and treasures of a defeated foe, or loot gathered by victorious soldiers. But *spoil* also means ruin or damage, and war is among the most ruinous of all human activities. Not only is it ruinous to human life and values but it is also destructive to the natural world. The human costs of war are so tragic that they often outshadow the damage done to nature, but some of the world's worst environmental disasters have been caused by war. In some cases environmental destruction has been an indirect by-product of warfare, akin to the trampling of fields by armies surging back and forth across them. Other cases, however, have involved deliberate environmental warfare: attacking an enemy by hurting that enemy's environment.

The link between war and environmental disaster is probably as old as warfare itself. Three thousand or more years ago, according to the Book of Judges in the Bible, chemical warfare was practiced in Jordan when the victorious army of Abimelech spread salt on the defeated city of Shechem to make it infertile and uninhabitable. Rome was said to have done the same thing in the second century B.C. to its great enemy, the North African city of Carthage.

Scorched-earth fighting is the tactic of making it impossible for an enemy to live off the land. By seizing or destroying crops, poisoning wells, killing livestock, and—in an age of more sophisticated technology—destroying railroads, hospitals, telegraph and telephone lines, power stations, and the like, an army can deprive its enemy of food, shelter, cover, and the ability to fight back. On rare occasions scorched-earth tactics have been used defensively, as when Napoleon Bonaparte invaded Russia in 1812 with 450,000 soldiers. The Russians steadily retreated, and Napoleon pursued them all the way to Moscow. But as the Russians withdrew from the advancing French army, they took with them all the food they could carry and destroyed the rest; they even killed wild animals so that the French would not be able to hunt for food. Russia withstood Napoleon's assault, and the French were forced to retreat for hundreds of miles through bitter weather, starving as they went. By the time he left Russia, Napoleon had barely 10,000 men left in fighting condition. The Russians' scorched-earth defense had worked. They had devastated a huge swath of their own landscape, but they did so deliberately in order to make things difficult for the invader.

More often, though, scorched-earth tactics are used offensively by one power to subdue or punish another. In the American Civil War, the North employed these methods against the South, especially in General William T. Sherman's march through Georgia in 1864, when he stripped fields, burned buildings, and generally tried to cripple not just the Confederate army but also the civilian life of the region through which he passed. In the 20th century, the British waged scorched-earth warfare against the Mau Mau rebels in Kenya in the 1950s; the French used the tactic against the Algerians from 1949 to 1962; and the former Soviet Union employed it during the Soviet invasion of Afghanistan in the 1980s. When the Soviets withdrew from Afghanistan, they left behind them a blighted land, greatly deforested by scorched-earth warfare, scarred with craters from bombs and shells. The landscape was littered with tangles of barbed wire, rusting gun emplacements and tanks, and thousands of land mines and unexploded shells that continued to claim the lives of unsuspecting farmers and children long after the last Russian soldiers had left the country.

In such cases, the primary goal is to kill or suppress the enemy, and destroying the environment is seen as a handy way to

*Thousands of drums of the defoliant Agent Orange were stored at the Naval Construction Battalion Center in Gulfport, Mississippi, for years after the Vietnam War ended. Disposal was a serious problem.*

accomplish that goal. In recent years the Ethiopian army has destroyed crops and grasslands to bring about famine in regions that resist Ethiopian rule; famine has also been used as a weapon in the Sudan and elsewhere. When Iraq's government used poison gas against Kurdish nationalists, the motive was not just to kill Kurds; the gas also damaged the vegetation in the Kurdish tribal districts so that the Kurds, whose economy was based on livestock herding, could not go on living there.

Occasionally war benefits the environment in unexpected ways—though usually for only a short while. For example, in the 1970s and 1980s, fighting between government forces and antigovernment guerrillas in Nicaragua halted the rapid spread of cattle ranching and of the timber industry in that Central American country. Some stands of rainforest that had been marked for destruction received a reprieve. And because peasants were afraid to be seen with hunting rifles lest they be taken for enemies and shot by either soldiers or guerrillas, the killing of wildlife diminished. Deer, jaguars, crocodiles, iguanas, and other animals that had been declining made a comeback. The same thing has happened in other zones of conflict when war has disrupted peacetime activities that were harmful to the environment. But these temporary gains are usually undone once the fighting stops. And certainly no one would recommend war as a form of environmental protection. It destroys infinitely more than it accidentally saves.

### ECOCIDE

The Vietnam War left many bitter legacies. It cost thousands of American lives and many more Vietnamese lives. It pitted various groups within American society against one another in angry, sometimes violent confrontations. It created a generation of war veterans who suffer from unique psychological stresses and physical illnesses. But it also devastated the environment of Vietnam, especially in the south, where U.S. forces battled the army of the Communist north and its southern sympathizers for more than a decade.

In Vietnam, Americans found themselves battling guerrillas and villagers as well as enemy soldiers. The favored tactic of the U.S. forces was air strikes. A historian of the U.S. Strategic Air Command wrote, "Guerrillas are not fought with rifles, but rather located and then bombed to oblivion." But the United States had a hard time locating the Vietnamese guerrillas; its motto became, "When in doubt, bomb." B-52 aircraft flew daily bombing runs over South Vietnam in what an American news broadcast called "the greatest concentration of mass firepower in the history of warfare." They dropped 13 million tons of bombs over 30% of South Vietnam's territory, creating a landscape pocked with more than 250 million raw, muddy bomb craters. As these holes filled with stagnant water, they became breeding places for disease-bearing mosquitoes. "Bomb-crater malaria" became a health hazard in areas where malaria had formerly been rare.

Bombing was not the only assault on the Vietnamese environment. U.S. forces were determined to defoliate—remove the foliage, or leaves, from—the forests that provided cover for the enemy. They accomplished this partly with specially modified tractors called Rome plows that sawed down and uprooted entire forests. But mostly they did it with herbicides, plant-killing chemicals that were sprayed on forests and croplands. Between

*Vietnam veterans in Washington, D.C., protest the government's lack of concern for their health problems.*

1961 and 1971 the United States sprayed more than 20 million gallons of herbicides on South Vietnam, destroying 14% of its forests and 8% of its croplands. The hardest-hit ecosystem was the mangrove forest that once lined most of Vietnam's coastline, where it sheltered many species of birds and animals and provided a nursery for thriving fish and shrimp populations. Half of the mangrove forests were destroyed by the herbicides. The most notorious of the herbicides was Agent Orange, a compound that contained highly toxic dioxin. Another compound, called Agent Blue, was sprayed on a million acres of rice-growing land. It contained arsenic, a deadly poison. In a bitter irony, these carcinogenic defoliating chemicals have caused deaths and illnesses among Americans who were exposed to them as well as among the Vietnamese.

The Americans did not win the war in Vietnam, despite the enormous scale of their assault on nature—an assault that gave rise to the term *ecocide,* which means "the killing of ecosystems." Another ecocide occurred in 1991, and this time it was an attack on nature by an army that had already lost the war.

The Persian Gulf War began when the Gulf nation of Iraq invaded neighboring Kuwait. A coalition of Kuwait's allies, headed by the United States, sent troops and military hardware to the Middle East to prevent the Iraqis from invading other countries and to drive them out of Kuwait. The war was short. A combination of high-technology air strikes against Iraq and a short but intense land war swept the Iraqis out of Kuwait and forced Iraq's surrender in less than six weeks. Before they left, however, the retreating Iraqis committed one of the most heinous acts of environmental sabotage in history. They dynamited 800 oil wells, 600 of which were set burning, and they blasted scores of oil pipelines, storage facilities, and loaded tankers. The result was the most severe environmental pollution the world has ever seen.

The Iraqis did not just scorch the earth. They stained the sea and turned the midday sky black with smoke. The plume of sooty smoke from the burning wells rose high into the sky and floated for hundreds of miles. Scientists feared that it might reach the jet stream, a belt of winds that rushes around the globe at 45,000 feet. The jet stream could have carried soot and chemicals from the burning oil all over the world, contributing to pollution and perhaps affecting global weather. The plume, however, never rose above 22,000 feet. Although skiers in India's Kashmir state, in the western Himalayas, reported oily soot on the snow, most of the plume's effects were limited to the Gulf nations. The fires and smoke created high concentrations of hazardous chemicals such as carbon dioxide and sulfur dioxide, as well as tons of soot. Yet the pollution was less severe than experts had initially feared. A hundred miles or so from the sources of the fires, which were clustered near the head of the Gulf, levels of most contaminants were close to U.S. air quality standards.

Putting out oil fires is hazardous and highly specialized work. Faced with more than 600 such fires, officials at first feared that it would take years to put them all out. This dire prediction was wrong. Thanks to the extraordinary efforts of fire-fighting crews from many nations, all fires were extinguished and all leaking wells were capped by November 1991, less than a year after the war began. By then, however, large areas of fragile desert terrain and once-fertile gardens had been heavily coated by hot, oily particles that had fallen from the sky. Long-term studies will be needed to identify other possible legacies of the fire, such as an increase in respiratory diseases among the people of Kuwait and Saudi Arabia, or acid rain in the Middle East caused by increased sulfur dioxide in the atmosphere.

While the fires were darkening the sky, millions of gallons of oil were leaking from damaged wells, ships, pipelines, and storage tanks in what was by far the biggest oil spill ever. Some of this oil pumped out onto the land, where it formed vast, gleaming black lakes and threatened groundwater supplies. But the bulk of it went into the Persian Gulf. The exact amount of oil that was spilled is unknown, but it is estimated to have been between 6 and 8 million barrels—that is, between a quarter and a third of a billion gallons. (The spill could have been more than twice as large, but four clever Kuwaitis falsified a valve reading on storage tanks at the Sea Island Terminal that held another 8.5 million barrels of oil. This ruse tricked the Iraqi saboteurs into thinking they had emptied those tanks, which in fact remained sealed.) Some of the spilled oil belonged to Iraq, not Kuwait, which only underscores the meaninglessness of the destruction. "Strategically it was senseless," said Abdullah Toukan, science adviser to Jordan's King Hussein. "The only casualty was the environment."

The Persian Gulf was scarcely pristine even before the sabotage. Many oil-drilling operations are located along its shores, and a great part of the world's petroleum shipping passes through its waters. These activities have been polluting the Gulf for years. Each year, an average of 250,000 barrels of

*An engraving of Civil War general William Tecumseh Sherman, one of the first generals in history to practice total war against a civilian population.*

War in Ethiopia, Somalia, and the Sudan has accelerated the degradation of the land begun by natural causes such as drought.

oil—roughly equal to the amount spilled in the *Valdez* disaster—are spilled or discharged into the Gulf. The sheer magnitude of the Iraqis' spill, however, overwhelmed attempts to contain it. Efforts were made to save birds, rare sea turtles, and mammals imperiled by the spill, but many delicate shallow-water habitats along the coast of Saudi Arabia were fouled by oil. Experts estimate that about half the oil eventually evaporated. Perhaps 2 million barrels were salvaged and stored in large desert pits. Only time will tell what effects the rest of the oil will have on the already overstressed water and wildlife of the Persian Gulf. Environmentalists hope that the shock of the severe spill has alerted the people of the Gulf nations to the need to protect the waterway from smaller, everyday spills and leaks. Already the 1991 disaster has spurred the establishment of marine parks and sanctuaries in critical Gulf habitats.

Oceanographer Sylvia A. Earle, who during the Gulf War was the chief scientist of the U.S. National Oceanic and Atmospheric Administration, made four trips to Kuwait and Saudi Arabia to assess the environmental impact of the war. She pointed out the need for continuing cooperation among the world's scientists in the face of assaults on the environment. "Research will continue in the Gulf, as scientists monitor the interplay of air, land, and sea and work to accelerate the region's restoration," she wrote in 1992. "The knowledge gained may help win peace with the environment—one small but precious dividend of a costly war."

*Vice-President Albert Gore, who has made the environment a major concern, is widely viewed as the best hope for a more environmentally responsible political agenda during the Clinton administration.*

# PREVENTING
# ENVIRONMENTAL
# DISASTERS

Disasters such as Love Canal, the Bhopal leak, the Chernobyl explosion, and the *Valdez* spill have outraged and alarmed people all over the world. They have prompted a widespread demand for tighter controls on the oil, nuclear, and chemical industries and for efforts to clean up existing toxic messes. Not many years ago, environmentalism was of interest only to a small segment of the population, and conservationists were dismissed as "tree-huggers." Now, however, concern for the environment has moved into the mainstream of life in many countries, including the United States. One symbol of this shift is Albert Gore, a former U.S. senator noted for his interest in environmental issues. In 1989, addressing a gathering of world leaders, he said that rescuing the environment will become the "new 'sacred agenda' in international affairs." Gore became the vice president of the United States in 1993; his supporters hope that this accession marks a new American commitment to the environment.

It is probably impossible to prevent environmental disasters altogether. Total prevention would demand a radical transformation of the world economy and of the way people live. For example, habits of production and consumption requiring large quantities of oil and chemicals are deeply ingrained in the Western way of life and are becoming the norm around the world. Yet perhaps the frequency, as well as the severity, of disasters can be reduced. Every disaster that has occurred has taught us something about how it might have been prevented. With care and cooperation, the nations of the world can avert many potential disasters, thus saving lives and preventing crippling blows to the earth's ecosystems. We have also learned

*Reducing air pollution may require higher gasoline prices, more expensive electric cars, and many other measures that will make the automobile less attractive to American consumers.*

much about how best to respond to disasters. The experience gained by relief workers in Chernobyl, Prince William Sound, Kuwait, and elsewhere is part of a growing global arsenal of knowledge that can help us minimize the effects of new disasters while we clean up the residues of old ones. All that is needed is for governments, corporations, and communities to insist that safety be the highest priority in every potentially hazardous undertaking.

One thing that has been clearly demonstrated by the environmental disasters of the 1970s, 1980s, and 1990s is that individuals and small groups *can* make a difference. NIMBYs have shut down old nuclear reactors and forestalled the building of new ones. They have forced the cleanup of toxic wastes and have initiated the passage of environmental laws at the local, state, and federal levels. They have lost some battles, but they have won many others. As American anthropologist Margaret Mead, a member of many environmental organizations, once said, "Never doubt that a small group of thoughtful, committed citizens can change the world. Indeed, it's the only thing that ever has."

## THINGS EVERYONE CAN DO NOW

- Make an environmental disaster the subject of a school project or report.
- Write to the manufacturers of chemical products you use—cosmetics or grooming aids, paints, bug sprays, and the like—to express your views about reducing and managing toxic waste.

*The electric car, still in the experimental stage, does not pollute the air, but its engineering is complex and its range is limited.*

○ Reduce your consumption of petroleum-based products such as gasoline. When possible, walk or take public transportation instead of driving. Choose products made of cloth, metal, or recyclable paper over plastic products (plastics contain petrochemicals).

○ Reduce your exposure to pesticides—and show that you would like to see their use diminished. Ask your grocer to carry untreated, organic produce.

○ If there is a nuclear power plant in your area, find out whether it offers public tours of the facility. Ask about the plant's safety record, and about where and how its nuclear waste is stored. Show the nuclear industry that you are concerned about possible human health and environmental hazards.

- Study the publications of organizations that work to improve environmental conditions and prevent disasters: environmental groups, peace groups, antinuclear groups. Find an organization whose goals you support, and make a contribution of your time or money.
- When you use or dispose of environmentally hazardous materials such as bleach, motor oil, nail polish remover, and batteries, do so safely. Such materials should be taken to a toxic substance disposal facility; your city or state environmental department can tell you where the closest one is located.

*Organic fruits and vegetables, grown without chemical fertilizers, pesticides, or herbicides, are becoming increasingly popular with American consumers.*

- Are there current environmental controversies in your community—protests over nuclear sites, for example, or hearings about dump closings? Follow the development of local issues that might be related to environmental disasters. Attend a public meeting. If you feel strongly about an environmental issue, prepare a petition to deliver to local, state, or federal authorities and collect signatures.
- The newspapers, as well as the publications of environmental organizations, can keep you informed about bills being considered in Congress that might effect the environment. Write to your senator or congressperson to express your support of or opposition to a proposed bill dealing with oil exploration, chemical safety, or energy.
- Where the well-being of the environment is concerned, one of the most important things we can all do is to learn from our mistakes. Reviewing the blighting effects of the Persian Gulf War, William Reilly, head of the Environmental Protection Agency, said, "Terrible as the disaster was, much greater would be the tragedy if we did not learn from it." Those fitting words apply to every environmental disaster the earth and its inhabitants have endured.

# APPENDIX: FOR MORE INFORMATION

## Environmental Organizations

Canadian Nature Federation
453 Sussex Drive
Ottawa, Ontario
Canada K1N 6Z4
(613) 238-6154

Center for Science in the Public
  Interest
1501 16th Street NW
Washington, DC 20036
(202) 332-9110

Citizen's Clearinghouse
  for Hazardous Waste
P.O. Box 926
Arlington, VA 22216
(703) 276-7070

Environmental Defense
  Fund
257 Park Avenue South
New York, NY 10010
(212) 505-2100

Greenpeace
1436 U Street NW
Washington, DC 20009
(202) 462-1177

League of Conservation Voters
1150 Connecticut Street NW
Washington, DC 20036
(202) 785-8683

National Audubon Society
950 Third Avenue
New York, NY 10022
(212) 832-3200

National Wildlife Federation
1400 16th Street NW
Washington, DC 20036
(202) 797-6800

Natural Resources Defense
  Council
40 West 20th Street
New York, NY 10011
(212) 727-2700

Sierra Club
730 Polk Street
San Francisco, CA 94109
(415) 776-2211

U.S. Public Interest Research
  Group
215 Pennsylvania Avenue SE
Washington, DC 20003
(202) 546-9707

## Government Agencies

Consumer Product Safety
  Commission
6 World Trade Center
New York, NY 10048
(212) 264-1125

Department of Energy
1000 Independence Avenue SW
Washington, DC 20585
(202) 586-5000

Environmental Protection Agency
401 M Street SW
Washington, DC 20460
(202) 382-2090

Federal Energy Regulatory
  Commission
825 North Capitol Street NE
Washington, DC 20426
(202) 357-8200

PICTURE CREDITS

AP/Wide World Photos: pp. 24, 94; The Bettmann Archive: pp. 12, 91; © Bettye-Lane: p. 75; S.C. Delancey/U.S. EPA: pp. 26, 28, 99; Department of Energy: p. 98; Courtesy Department of Library Services, American Museum of Natural History: pp. 15 (neg. no. 324410), 22 (neg. no. 282680); Federal Highway Administration, U.S. Department of Transportation: p. 96; © Buddy Mays/Travel Stock: p. 79; NASA: p. 17; Reuters/Bettmann: pp. 20, 46, 52, 62, 66, 69, 72, 92; UPI/Bettmann: pp. 23, 31, 32, 33, 34, 39, 43, 48, 55, 58, 60, 82, 85, 88.

# FURTHER READING

Bergin, Edward, and Ronald Grandon. *How To Survive in Your Toxic Environment.* New York: Avon, 1984.

Brown, Michael. *Laying Waste: The Poisoning of America by Toxic Chemicals.* New York: Pantheon, 1980.

Bulloch, David. *The Wasted Ocean.* New York: Lyons and Burford, 1989.

Caplan, Ruth. *Our Earth, Ourselves.* New York: Bantam Books, 1990.

Carr, Terry. *Spill! The Story of the Exxon Valdez.* New York: Franklin Watts, 1991.

Carson, Rachel. *The Edge of the Sea.* Boston: Houghton Mifflin, 1955.

———. *Silent Spring.* Boston: Houghton Mifflin, 1962.

Edwards, Mike. "Chernobyl: One Year After." *National Geographic,* May 1987, pp. 632–53.

Epstein, Samuel, Lester Brown, and Carl Pope. *Hazardous Waste in America.* San Francisco: Sierra Club Books, 1982.

Feshbach, Murray, and Alfred Friendly. *Ecocide in the U.S.S.R.* New York: Basic Books, 1992.

Global Tomorrow Coalition. *Global Ecology Handbook.* Boston: Beacon Press, 1990.

Gordon, Ben, and Peter Montague. *Zero Discharge: A Citizen's Toxic Waste Manual.* Washington: Greenpeace, 1989.

Hawley, T. M. *Against the Fires of Hell.* New York: Harcourt Brace Jovanovich, 1992.

Hunter, Linda Mason. *The Healthy Home: An Attic-to-Basement Guide to Toxin-Free Living.* Emmaus, PA: Rodale Press, 1989.

League of Women Voters. *Nuclear Waste Primer.* Washington: League of Women Voters, 1985.

Lee, Douglas. "Tragedy in Alaska Waters." *National Geographic,* August 1989, pp. 260–63.

Moore, Andrew O. *Making Polluters Pay.* Washington: Environmental Action Foundation, 1987.

Naar, Jon. *Design for a Livable Planet: How You Can Help Clean Up the Environment.* New York: Harper & Row, 1990.

National Wildlife Federation. *Reducing the Risk of Chemical Disaster.* Washington: National Wildlife Federation, 1989.

Nietschmann, Bernard, and others. "The Ecology of War and Peace." *Natural History,* November 1990, pp. 34–49.

Ornstein, Robert, and Paul Ehrlich. *New World, New Mind.* New York: Simon & Schuster, 1989.

Puch, David I. *Radiation Alert.* New York: Doubleday, 1985.

Regenstein, Lewis. *How To Survive in America the Poisoned.* Washington: Acropolis Books, 1986.

Salisbury, Harrison. *The Great Black Dragon Fire: A Chinese Inferno.* Boston: Little, Brown, 1989.

Shabecoff, Philip. *A Fierce Green Fire: The American Environmental Movement.* New York: Hill & Wang, 1993.

Simon, Anne. *Neptune's Revenge.* New York: Franklin Watts, 1984.

Steger, Will, and Jon Bowermaster. *Saving the Earth: A Citizen's Guide to Environmental Action.* New York: Knopf, 1990.

Stephens, Sharon. "Lapp Life after Chernobyl." *Natural History,* December 1987, pp. 32–41.

Weiner, Jonathan. *The Next One Hundred Years: Shaping the Fate of Our Living Earth.* New York: Bantam Books, 1990.

Weir, David. *The Bhopal Syndrome.* San Francisco: Sierra Club Books, 1987.

Winckler, Suzanne. *Our Endangered Planet.* Minneapolis: Lerner, 1991.

World Resources Institute. *The 1992 Information Please Environmental Almanac.* Boston: Houghton Mifflin, 1992.

Readers can gain a better understanding of both scientific and political aspects of the issues surrounding environmental disasters by searching out past, present, and future issues of the magazines *Hazardous Waste News, Right-to-Know News, Ocean Watch,* and *Toxic Times.*

# GLOSSARY

**carcinogen**   Something that causes cancer.

**contaminant**   A substance that contaminates something else, or makes it unfit to use.

**ecocide**   The destruction of **ecosystems;** an assault on the environment.

**ecosystem**   An interrelated, interdependent community of living creatures and their habitat.

**emission**   Something that is emitted, or discharged; usually used to refer to gases, radiation, or particles emitted into the air, but can also refer to liquids.

**hazardous**   Dangerous; may be flammable, explosive, or **toxic.**

**herbicide**   Something used to kill plants; often used to refer to chemical sprays.

**NIMBY**   "Not In My Back Yard"—the slogan used by grass-roots activists to oppose waste dumps, nuclear plants, and **toxic emissions** in their communities; activist groups are sometimes called NIMBYs.

**pesticide**   Something used to kill pests such as insects and rodents; often used to refer to chemical sprays.

**toxic**   Poisonous. See **toxin.**

**toxin**   Poison; sometimes used to refer to chemicals that may be considered safe in very small amounts under controlled circumstances but are deadly when uncontrolled, as in waste dumps.

# I N D E X

## ABOUT THE AUTHOR

REBECCA STEFOFF is a Portland-based freelance writer and editor who has published more than 40 nonfiction books for young adults. Many of her books deal with geography and exploration, and she takes an active interest in environmental issues and global ecology. She has also served as the editorial director of Chelsea House's *Places and Peoples of the World* and *Let's Discover Canada* series. Stefoff received her M.A. and Ph.D. degrees in English from the University of Pennsylvania, where she taught for three years.

## ABOUT THE EDITOR

RUSSELL E. TRAIN, currently chairman of the board of directors of the World Wildlife Fund and The Conservation Foundation, has had a long and distinguished career of government service under three presidents. In 1957 President Eisenhower appointed him a judge of the United States Tax Court. He served Lyndon Johnson on the National Water Commission. Under Richard Nixon he became under secretary of the Interior and, in 1970, first chairman of the Council on Environmental Quality. From 1973 to 1977 he served as administrator of the Environmental Protection Agency. Train is also a trustee or director of the African Wildlife Foundation; the Alliance to Save Energy; the American Conservation Association; Citizens for Ocean Law; Clean Sites, Inc.; the Elizabeth Haub Foundation; the King Mahendra Trust for Nature Conservation (Nepal); Resources for the Future; the Rockefeller Brothers Fund; the Scientists' Institute for Public Information; the World Resources Institute; and Union Carbide and Applied Energy Services, Inc. Train is a graduate of Princeton and Columbia Universities, a veteran of World War II, and currently resides in the District of Columbia.